Carefree Black Boy:

Essays on Life and Redefining Masculinity

Sampson McCormick

With an Introduction by Darryl Stephens

This is a small token of encouragement for little black boys hiding in the darkness of closets, and men hiding in the shadows of shame. A gift for those who continue to soldier on in love and determination of creating a better world, full of opportunity, equality, laughter, joy and humanity. My honest feelings for those who want to learn a little more, just to feel normal, or relate to those who are a little different than they are.

It had been over five years since my last written project that didn't involve me preparing material for the stage, or content for a film or screen project. My life in the last few years has gone through lots of twists and turns, some that I didn't think I'd make it through, and more than once found me at the edge of frightening places. However, I'm grateful for humor, faith, weed, good friends, the stage, gospel, and house music. You see, as a stand-up comic, someone who uses humor on stage, to confront some challenging realities that I face not only as a human being, but a man who is black, and happens to be gay, I feel like some people forget the process of creating art, and the different places that it can come from, some are funny, in fact many are, but I've come out of a period where I'd get standing ovations night after night, and return to a life, where not much was funny to me at all. Despite the challenges, some that you'll read in this book, others I've shared on stage, and some that I'll feel comfortable enough, or time will be ripe enough to share later, I'm still here... and so are you.

Contents

Carefree Black Boys

By Darryl Stephens

"Carefree Black Boys" weren't officially a thing when I was growing up. In the world before social media, a movement celebrating young black men for existing outside the restrictive parameters of American manliness seemed beyond our collective imagination. Sure, we had Prince shimmying and split kicking through every boundary the white patriarchy could place in his path, but he was so otherworldly and impossible to peg that at the time, many of us didn't even know he was ours to claim. The fact that straight women found his ruffled blouses, high heeled boots, and eyeliner sexually enticing was probably more confusing than empowering for gay boys like me who were struggling to find images affirming our "otherness."

A handful of openly queer black dance music artists (Sylvester, Jermaine Stewart, Kevin Aviance, among others) offered glimpses of how gender and sexuality could be reimagined on the nightclub stage. However, for those of us still living with our parents, they weren't the easiest role models to emulate... Not without getting our asses kicked. Today, the children have Kid Cudi rocking crop tops before hip-hop stadium crowds, Jaden Smith modeling women's clothes in Louis Vuitton ads, Odell Beckham, Jr. splashing around in hot tubs with other shirtless football players under a crown of blond curls, and Frank Ocean singing dreamy love songs about boys. Barry Jenkins' gorgeous black gay film Moonlight won the Academy Award for Best Picture and one of the film's stars, Ashton Sanders, attended the Vanity Fair Oscar after-party in a kilt, skullcap, and Vans sneakers. The world is changing, and for those of us who were forging queer identities before Jussie Smollett's character on

Empire and before Beyoncé was posting Instagram videos celebrating marriage equality, the shifts feel pretty monumental, that doesn't mean we don't still have a ways to go.

Too many of our own–from professional athletes to popular music artists to respected religious leaders–consider the visibility of openly gay Black folks and gender non-conforming Black people detrimental to the very fabric of African-American culture and society. They have bought into the white supremacist notion that Black masculinity should be based squarely in displays of brute strength and unwavering emotional detachment. They believe we should not be allowed to be sensitive or compassionate or artistic. Black men are instead socialized to dominate and disrespect Black women, encouraged to insult and commit violence against individuals who challenge their conventional views of gender, and taught to deny any sexual impulse that doesn't directly lead to overpopulation. The insidious "Christian" colonization of the Black psyche has pit families against their queer children and led to countless murders of LGBT-identified Black people. Obviously, this divisiveness does nothing to strengthen the Black community; instead, it weakens our sense of autonomy and dilutes our cultural impact by tearing us apart.

This is not a new tactic; the 'divide and conquer' strategy has always allowed those in power–the very wealthy minority–to maintain control over their subjects–the overworked and struggling majority–by sowing fear and suspicion among each subordinate group to scare them from joining forces and overthrowing the ruling class. When women, people of color, religious minorities, LGBT folks, and poor people finally recognize that we are all "queer" in the eyes of rich white men… as soon as we start accepting and utilizing our intersectionality as momentum toward coalition building…when we stop projecting their bigotry onto each other and ourselves, that is when we will rise. Only then will we win.

One of the most powerful ways we can open and change minds is by living authentically and without shame. Any preconceived notions of who we are supposed to be can effectively be erased by the truth of how we function in our personal relationships and in our day-to-day lives. Honoring all of our contradictions and complexities affirms our humanity, strengthens our integrity, and gives us the space to develop the emotional intelligence to love one another and to love ourselves. Our freedom demands that we recognize each other for who we are, rather than what the world has been socialized to see.

Sampson McCormick has been entertaining and enlightening people from all walks of life with his candid brand of comedy for sixteen years. He's made a name for himself in the straight white male-dominated standup world, boldly carving out his own path by owning and embracing his Black gay experience with insightful humor and raw honesty. As sassy and salacious as he is scholarly, he consistently manages to skewer subjects like racism and homophobia with startling wisdom and biting wit. He challenges audiences to rethink their preconceptions by simply being true to himself, and in doing so, he invites us all to be more confident in our own self-expression.

This is why Carefree Black Boys are such a crucial component to dismantling the myth of white supremacy. In a nation that seeks to vilify all African-American men as debauched deadbeats and/or violent criminals, Black boys dancing to house music in see-through caftans, or wearing flowers in their beards, or discussing mental health challenges on Twitter, or holding hands while walking down the street are nothing short of revolutionary. Carefree Black Boys are not beholden to the fear-based bullshit we've all been fed about ethnic inferiority or the tragedy of emasculation. They are pierced septum poets, tattooed comic book nerds, blue-haired baristas, openly gay gospel singers, and standup comics flaunting go-go dancer physiques. They are unburdened, unbothered, and unapologetic. They are the future of Black manhood. And the future is free baby!

1. "Do You, Boo"

(from message delivered at Metropolitan Community Church in Coachella Valley, CA

—June 2013)

I'm a product of what some may refer to as "The Ghetto", those of us who've lived there referred to it more affectionately, as "The Hood", or "around the way", I feel like it helped to take the sting out of the labels and connotations associated with where we just so happened to live, and we knew that many people didn't view living in "the ghetto", as a good thing. Many, hear that word and think of a poor section of a city inhabited primarily by people of the same race or social background. Many people think of violence, poverty, childhood pregnancies, lack of education, people sitting around on the front porch wearing flip flops, smoking cigarettes, being loud, eating crabs and tuna fish sandwiches. I know one of the good things about the kind of neighborhood I grew up in, is that sometimes it kept me away from people who I didn't really want to be bothered with, every now and again, I'd have some crazy guy, who'd want to take me on a date, and I knew that if anything else I said, couldn't get me out of it, I knew that whenever I'd tell them what area of the city I lived in, they'd go "Oh, no! I'm not coming over there."

But regardless of what people had to say about where we were from, we knew differently. And because of the way that some of us had grown up, our affections toward one another weren't the standard hugs, and back rubs and kisses. Sometimes, it was something simple, like jumping rope and playing double-dutch, sitting down and sharing some fish and French Fries, and I'm not ashamed to say, sometimes just sitting around laughing and passing a joint. Many of us didn't know how to quote Langston Hughes, Maya Angelou or Audre Lorde, yet we still found ways to affirm and encourage one another. If you saw somebody looking good, telling them, "You've got it going on!" or if somebody was trying to pull you down, having your best friend tell you "Shake the haters off." But my favorite expression was "Do You, Boo." This meant many things. "Don't worry about what's going on around you, just focus on you." "It doesn't matter what anybody has to say about what you like, if you like it and they don't, then that's their problem."

As many of us got older, and began to strive for better lives, we found that this meant something even greater. To me, being able to take that expression and run with it, meant that regardless of what anybody had to say about what way that your life should go. And I thought to title this encouragement "Do You, Boo."

"You have to go the way that your blood beats. If you don't live the only life that you have, you won't live some other life you won't live any life at all."

-James Baldwin

Let us take a moment, to reflect on that quote from what I like to call the gospel of James Baldwin, and ask ourselves how often do we really live life? How often do we go the way that our blood beats? I feel like many of us, have gotten lost in the routine of simply waking up every day, merely existing, and often times, trying to live the way that other people say that we should live, whether it be trying to keep up with the Joneses, or living in a certain box. But, how many of are truly experiencing, embracing, and most of all really taking moments to appreciate this gift that we've been given, called life? When are you finally going to take a moment to "Do YOU, boo?" How many of us are allowing ourselves to take the time and or learn to finally breathe through our own nostrils, speak with our own mouths, think with our own heads, and see through our own eyes? I feel like, because of what we've been taught, and sometimes simply being afraid, we can end up going through life on puppet strings or living in a comatose state.

Uniqueness and individuality are the special things that make each and every one of us stand out in our true divine originality, but we've been manipulated into wasting our time, entertaining and being taunted by what we see in film, on television, what we're told by society, our peers, our closest relatives and friends, even the church, when they tell us that who we are, what we look like, where we live and how or who we love, are things to regret, loathe or be ashamed of. The only thing worse than us hearing these things, is that even more often, than we hear it, we believe it. But when are you going to take a moment to realize, that you've got to "Do YOU, boo?"

Too many of us, have merely existed, ingesting toxic messages and allowing people who shouldn't, to have power over our lives, because we've been believing that everybody else's opinions about us matter, when in reality, unless it's an opinion that comes from GOD or Oprah, then it really shouldn't make a difference. But we hear these things, and live in fear of ourselves, of life, of one another and living up to our fullest potentials. Isn't it sad to think, that we can make decisions to never fully embellish our lives?

How many of us, are really standing up and taking our lives back, embracing the possibilities of our greatness and eliminating the restrictions that have been placed on our freedom? How many of us are shaking free of the chains that have been placed on our minds and hearts, the very barriers that prevent us from loving one another, most of all, ourselves? I think it was RuPaul who said "If you can't love yourself, then how in the hell can you love somebody else?" But again, how can we love ourselves, if we learn to become a person who isn't authentic to who it is that we really are? "Do YOU, boo!"

I think that it's funny to live in a society that critiques authenticity, yet glorifies the travesty that is reality television. And I'm not going to play innocent, and act like I don't indulge, because, I'm guilty of it. I just can't resist "Keeping Up with the Kardashians", "Real Housewives of Atlanta", "Love & Hip Hop". It's some of the most inhumane, non-sense garbage that you could ever see, and I'm tuned in for every episode. And I know I'm not the only one. But have you ever thought about the fact that we live in a society that views this as normal behavior, and turns around and judges real human beings?

Perhaps, we've never taken the time to really look at the condition of the world around us. Maybe the level of instability and craziness, has simply evolved and come to a place where, because so much is going on in this fast paced and busy world, that we've once again found a new way to normalize that, while we live in fear of what's real and that's our feelings, our dignity, hopes, dreams and desires. Do you realize that because of what we were told as children, what society tells us now, or what we even begin to tell ourselves and trick ourselves into believing that we really neglect the possibilities of greatness that we can allow GOD to help us bring into our lives? We live in a society that tells us constantly, what we can't make happen, and we internalize that, but we live in a day where kindergartners have higher IQ's than some politicians, people are on television and the internet, getting famous for eating cinnamon and having bronchitis, having careers, and making millions. Then surely, age can't stop you from going back to school for a degree, or where you come from affect where you are going, or just you, simply being able to stand up and live, embracing your possibilities, and being the person that you've been blessed and made by GOD to be.

One of the most beautiful things that I've learned, and sometimes, still have to remind myself of, is that we aren't just a product of a union that occurred between our parents, according to Psalms 139:13-14, which tells us that "we were knit together in our mother's womb. And that we should rejoice, for we've been fearfully and wonderfully made." This means that each and every one of us is a divine creation, chosen for this moment right now, and in GOD there are no failures or mistakes. We are fierce and fabulous, and have been made to shine, as bright beacons of hope, light and love in this world. Every day, we have to remember to remind ourselves of that, when we open our eyes, when we're brushing our teeth, washing our behinds, and getting all dressed up, smiling and looking sexy, that we've got to go out and remind our brothers and sisters that we encounter in the world. Too many people are hurting, ashamed of themselves and living in fear of letting the light shine on their face.

And I thank GOD, that I'm able to testify and know that it doesn't matter where you come from, it doesn't matter what direction that people send you in, or what they say about who you are, that GOD makes no mistakes. It doesn't matter that I'm black, when GOD gave me this brown skin, it was divine order. GOD put it on me, and made it beautiful. It doesn't matter that I'm gay. I know that GOD makes no mistakes. I remember growing up in a church, where the pastor preached against gay people and said that we were evil and did very bad things. And what hurts me even more, is that some of our gay, lesbian and transgender brothers and sisters, allow these seeds of hatred to grow inside of them, and it grows into self-loathing. Many of us live in fear of ourselves, not because we should be, but because we've been lied to, and we lie to ourselves. Some of us, because of this fear, live double lives, creating two and three email addresses and Facebook pages, one where we can be gay, and one where we can live an illusion. And that hurts me. And we cannot allow one another to continue to do the disservice to ourselves. We have to reach out to the people that we love, and tell them "If you are sitting in a church where they preach anything other than love and affirming the dignity of all people, and preach against you for who or how you love, GET UP, out of the choir stands, off the usher boards, out the pews, the pastor's lap, or wherever you are, and take your gay, lesbian, transgender tithes and offerings and walk up out of there!!!" It needs to be said over and over and over again, and a few times after that.

My GOD is NOT a GOD, who throws people into hell. I don't live in fear of the divine being of love and grace who created me perfectly to be who I am. I am fearfully and wonderfully made. I will not live in fear of myself, how I'm made, HATE FILLED interpretation of GOD, or ignorance. You can keep that because I won't be having it.

GOD's LOVE is unconditional, unlimited and complete.

When GOD got the idea to create each and every one of us, it was no mistake. We have to stand in love and humanity and never let anyone dictate the life that we have to live. We must be free and continue to shine bright until our lights reach the four corners of the earth and beyond that, that we are all beautifully and wonderfully made. Now is the time to stand up against hatred, and bullying, and stand up against hate crimes, intolerance, violence, injustice and to self-loathing. We can no longer be affected by the negativity that we are being fed. We must remember to go the way that our blood beats. There are over 7 billion people in this world and only one you. That's divine. We can no longer believe or feed the things that prevent us from living our best lives, being our best selves. We must embrace the possibilities and hold on to our faith. You've got to stay strong, love yourself and "Do YOU, Boo!" Amen and Ashe'.

2. *My Sex Positive*
Guardian Angel

Here I sat in a Whitman Walker Clinic testing room, two weeks before my 21st birthday, holding back tears of fear and regret, being consoled by the counselor as I rocked back and forth, tapping my foot nervously, watching the timer countdown the 20 minutes that I had to wait for the results of my first HIV test.

I was 20 years old and just getting my first taste of the gay nightlife. To my best friends, my getting out to the clubs, parties and "sexing" at what I now look back at, and consider a tender age made me a "late bloomer". They'd lost their virginity and were sneaking in bars by the time they were 14. I on the other hand was a "little church boy", sheltered by a strict, southern upbringing and had a 730PM curfew. I remember being out with my friends early Saturday evenings, constantly checking my watch for 630PM, which is when I'd scramble off, to go get home on time. Part of me wanted to buck my mother's and "Lord's" for that matter, authority, but the guilt of possibly disappointing my mother, and the anxiety brought on hearing our pastors speak of GOD's punishment (particularly AIDS for those who indulged in "the homosexual lifestyle" kept me in check.

It was my best friend, who one night, tired of me running off, and being afraid to begin experiencing life on my own terms, demanded an explanation. When I finally explained it to him, he laughed in my face "Indulge. Really? Is being gay high in calories or something?" He took my cell phone and turned it off, and unhooked the watch off my wrist, so I couldn't constantly check the time, and complain about how late it was getting. The sounds of some mega-diva dance mix came blasting out of the bar, "You hear that?" That's GOD telling you to get a life!" That night, we stayed out until 5AM, and I got to experience everything that I'd been missing, it was fabulous. My mother, realizing that I was grown, decided to, at the churches advice, "Turn me over to GOD", and let me start staying out. She did so reluctantly, so of course it was just *THAT* simple, before I'd go out, I would get hollered and prayed over, anointed oil slapped across my forehead, and each Sunday warned that "God was going to deal with me. Woe unto those who buck his almighty rule." While the back of my mind was cautious of the warning, I was happy to finally have freedom.

This freedom allowed me to dance without inhibitions until the wee hours of the morning, and finally see, flirt and be flirted with by the boys. I remember being approached by a dude on the dance floor at "The Edge", a very fondly remembered, now defunct gay club that once housed some of the best Friday night dance parties in the Navy Yard area of Washington, DC. Men, of all kinds, shirtless, gyrating, grinding on each other filled the place with exciting and highly sexual energy. I was by the front stage, gettin' it, having the time of my life. He came up behind me, and joined me in my dance, one I turned around to make sure he wasn't ugly, (I didn't wanna be surprised when the lights in the club came on), our bodies moved in a joint rhythm. We finally struck up a light, yet highly tantalizing conversation, my excitement, which I assumed was only "subtle", must have betrayed me, because he found it easy to ask for my phone number, and even easier to invite me to his place the next day.

I couldn't have been more ecstatic, my first "date" with someone I'd met at a club—cheesy, I know, but I'd finally get to share my own story about our nakedness, the way our tongues danced around in each other's mouths and the fact that I finally had a taste of the fun that my friends had such intriguing stories about. I floated on a cloud for about a week, feeling sexy and looking forward to more opportunities to "play catch up". That is, until I woke up with a cold, one worse than anything that had come to mind until then. Of course this freaked me out, and me, being the ultimate hypochondriac that I am, thought that I was dying, and did the worst possible thing that anyone could do to evaluate a health concern...googled my symptoms. After checking a few different things, I stumbled across what the symptoms could be pointing to, an HIV infection. I was absolutely terrified and immediately heard every sermon that I'd sat through, listening about how badly GOD punished gays. I battled anger and regret in my head and fingers, as I looked up testing sites in my area. The first one, was about three miles away, and accepted walk-ins. I took the trip, a 10 minute bus ride that seemed like a trip across the country, and finally there I was. It took everything to go through those doors, but I did.

Upon entering, I was greeted by the receptionist who asked about the purpose for my visit, and gave me a clipboard with two forms to fill out. Nervously, I completed them, and returned them to her. After a few minutes, my testing counselor, a tall, relaxed looking black woman walked towards me, a very welcoming smile on her face that immediately put me at ease. We walked into her office, where she introduced herself, Saadika, and explained to me that I should be proud of myself for coming to take the test. She went down a long list of questions, some that I felt too embarrassed to answer, and others that made us laugh. Finally, was the conversation about what brought me to her office, which was my recent hook up, and my paranoia, which she listened to without judgment. I guess she sensed that there had to be a deeper reasoning for my paranoia, which I finally explained "This was how GOD punished gay people." Her eyes were empathic, and she took my hand, "I can assure you, it's not. I could give you plenty of examples, but I prefer to keep loving energy flowing through my office. Let's just say that HIV isn't a punishment, and neither are cancer, diabetes, baldness, sickle cell or anything else. I'll start your test, and we will talk."

From there, she sanitized my middle finger, dried it and drew blood from the tip, reassuring me that it was almost over, as she administered the steps of the test, placed the kit, and set the timer, and now began the longest twenty minutes of my life. The first sixty seconds, doubled me over, and nearly reduced me to tears, and I thought several times about running out of there before the results were done. Saadika began to console me, and said something so outrageous, that I couldn't help but look at her like she was crazy. "GOD made sex for people to have, and people, means people, that means gay, straight and otherwise, and sex is good." I thought to myself, *this bitch done lost her mind*. She proceeded, "You're 21, and you're so uptight, getting laid more might be good for you...do you know why I'm so calm, so happy right now? It's because I had an orgasm last night. Am I encouraging you to be reckless? No. Use condoms, get tested regularly, every 4-6 months, have fun. Don't be afraid to use sex toys and explore your sexuality, it's perfectly okay, and I promise GOD isn't punishing you for anything. Once you start to get out and live, you'll understand how sex and divinity can go hand in hand." I asked how, she shrugged, "GOD works in mysterious ways. No matter what your result is today, you'll do what you need to do moving forward to take care of yourself, you're going to be just fine." Her phone rang, she picked up and excused herself from the office to walk into the waiting room to prep her next client.

She walked back in, just as the timer went off, silenced it, sat in her chair, and squeezed my hand, one last time, and promised me that either way, I would be fine. She gave me my result, and then smirked at me for a second, then said 'Will you make sure you penetrate somebody, or get penetrated next time, and then come back and see me? All these nerves are unnecessary for just a session where you spent an afternoon kissing, jerking off and dry humping." I looked at her and laughed, "Well, when you were asking me earlier and that's what I told you I've been doing, why didn't you say so?" She smiled that warm smile that made me comfortable with having her as my regular testing counselor, "It's my job to test you, no matter what you come in here and TELL me, silly, but I figured, you needed this moment."

With that, she gave me her business card, a hug and walked me to the door, where I came face to face with her next client, one of the pastors from my church who'd spent so many Sundays rebuking "sex demons", and besieging me to repent of homosexuality and what the repercussions would be if I didn't, there to get tested himself. We exchanged an awkward glance, one that was apparent enough to make Saadika raise her eyebrows as she escorted him into her office and closed the door. I couldn't believe it, all those Sundays I spent in guilt because "Sex was bad." And I'd be punished simply for being a human with desires, for just being me, praying for clarity one day, for answers that I was ok, and I wasn't doing anything wrong. Saadika was right, I needed that moment, to learn that sex is good, GOD doesn't "punish people with HIV or any other ailments", and sometimes, to quell your fears and let you know, will work in a mysterious way.

3. Friday Nights at Union Station

Although we aren't quite there yet, there's no denying that being gay now, socially at least, is a hell of a lot easier to be than it was 15, 10, even five years ago. It seems like just yesterday when the ideal image for a black, gay man to portray was the "DL Thug" type. Many of us spent so much of our time emulating tough guys, walking around in Timberland boots, sagging, baggy jeans, oversized basketball jerseys with fitted hats on backwards, no matter how much of a queen you might really be. From a distance, they might look like Meek Mill, but when they opened their mouths, or got in the bedroom, they sounded like Nicki Minaj. No matter though, it was all about the image. And between the image that was popular and the fact that we played dress up so that we wouldn't be subject to ridicule, especially those of us who lived in the hood and couldn't dare show that side of ourselves to our neighborhoods, friends and families, that was the thing and we did what we felt we had to do.

Fast forward to now, if you try to get a gay man to dress up like that, he'll give you an epic side eye, and a "Girl, Bye!" probably looking like Nicki Minaj, even if he sounds like Meek Mill. Things have drastically changed, where I remember a time when it seemed like you had to search for us, or be at a certain place at a particular time to find us, now, on streets and in work places, we are more visible than ever. When I'm traveling to places like New York, LA, Chicago, DC and especially, Atlanta, out and about at church, the movies, restaurants, parks or grocery stores, you see the black gays, out and in full force. When I'm out with my friends, I often joke and say "Damn! Is *EVERYBODY* gay now? I use to feel special. Pretty soon, straight people are gonna have to have pride parades." Although I say this only playfully—most of the time, I do believe that it's a testament to the fact that we now live in and get to experience a completely new existence of gay, lesbian and transgender folks.

Back in my teens, when my mom first started allowing me wiggle room to hang out with friends after school, I'd split my time between MLK library near Chinatown, and a mall/terminal in Washington, DC called Union Station. Both, much different places now than they were then, attracted all of "the kids". During the week, between the homeless people who hi-jacked the place as a shelter and the gay men who turned the basement bath and conference rooms into a glory hole, MLK library was everything except a place to go study and read books. So much went on in that library, to a point where looking back, I feel bad for that poor janitorial staff. They had a mess on their hands. Upstairs, especially on the very top level where all the heat from the building would rise up to, a whole lot of homeless people would congregate. There weren't many bathing options for them in the city, so the smell would get into the old vents and heating systems, and got on everything, in the carpet, walls, chairs, tables, and if you hung out in there too long, by the time you came out, you smelled like the elements. That smell was too much for some people walking in. I'd see lots of folks, especially women, battling the vestibule with perfume spray and finally giving up, and running back out, nearly in tears, overpowered by the funk.

Downstairs in the basement was a story of its own, kind of creepy upon first glance because the floors mostly, except in the hallway and conference rooms were concrete. It was dark, and you could hear folks shuffling about, the clinking of belt buckles from various corners of the stairwell and the conference rooms, and you didn't see anybody. You'd just be walking along and out of nowhere hear *"PSST...PSST!"* I was too scary to walk towards any of those sounds, and although I didn't have much experience "cruising", I did know enough I guess because of street smarts—maybe just plain common sense, that if someone was interested enough, they'd stop with the trick calls and come out and show their face and talk. Most of the time they did, and you'd be surprised who all was down there, people who worked on Capitol Hill, city council staffers, deacons and then there were bums and people who would suck you off, and while they were doing that, would slip your wallet out of your pocket and take all of your cash and credit cards, bitch, talk about talented and gifted. To think back on those days, that was pretty dangerous, but we got a thrill out of the experience. Every time you went down there, was something or someone new, although there were plenty of regulars.

I never had sex with anybody down there or put my mouth on anything, or any of that, but I would go watch and listen to the sounds, and if I got turned on any, and approached by someone, I might play with a scrotum or nipple or something, but I only did that two or three times. The dark conference rooms, stairwells and the bathroom furthest in the back of the basement was where all the action went down. Everything smelled like sex, sweat and cum, there would be used condoms kicked to the corners of the walls and some of everything else. Between the homeless people upstairs and the crazy stuff that went on downstairs, I'm surprised that the janitors didn't just give up and try to burn the place down one day. That library back in the day was an experience and a half.

At the end of the week, we all skipped the library and went straight to Union Station. On Friday nights, the place was electric, and attracted the who's who of the Washington, DC gay community. All the girls would come pomping through those corridors, in grand "Ya'll can't take me bitch!" fashion. I knew I was gay, and had a few sexual encounters with men, but socially, I didn't know what gay people did, or how they acted. From what I observed, all I could tell was that if you were gay, you were supposed to look fabulous and be loud. Believe me, I wasn't the only one who made this observation, because at 6PM it seemed like security started escorting all of the straight people out, and the gays took over from then until closing, which was round 1030PM. During those hours, I'd wander around aimlessly, just as innocent as I could be, looking at everybody in awe. These were people who I related to and couldn't take my eyes off of, but because I hadn't evolved to that level of expression quite yet, and it'd be years before I would, I knew that we were the same in some kind of way. I just couldn't quite figure out how. Of course, running with the adults and trying to see what they did, after a while my innocence became corrupted.

I say that in a good way because I enjoyed the experiences that I got to have at such a young age. I don't feel like LGBTQ youth of today get to have too many of the eye-opening, character building and fun experiences that previous generations got to enjoy. There's nothing to figure out, no sense of mystery in learning about your sexuality, clubs are harder to sneak into if you're under aged, and the biggest other two, there are more social media apps than I can name, or keep up with, and it's pure insanity that the folks who come to clubs and bars these days, after paying a $25 cover will interact with folks standing a few feet away from them on these apps, have to check to see if the person is on there, and if they aren't, don't have the gull to walk up and strike up a conversation, buy them a drink or ask for a dance, but I digress.

There are other things that I see when I go to gay clubs that have me (metaphorically) ready to gulp down my glass of house Merlot, pick up my purse and leave. Like when you go in and everybody is standing up on the wall, acting all hard, mean mugging and pretending to be trade (a man who could pass for heterosexual) until a Beyonce song comes on, then everybody breaks character, twerking on all fours, swinging their fitted hats as if it's an imaginary lace front wig, with their tongues hanging out of their head, screaming "Yassssss!" and carrying on. I guess that's one of the fun things about observing gay men too. There are so many different components to our personalities. While I do see many gay men do this in clubs, I think it's just more so fun to watch them break character. A gay man will always respond to his divas. At the same time, while I poke fun at this, I also encourage us to be as masculine and feminine as we can be. Why not embrace it all? What's the point of being gay if you can't do all the fun stuff? That's those poor macho, straight men who have to put themselves through that kind of agony. And I do believe that whether we are man or woman, gay or straight, we have both of those energies to call on when we need to. I feel like although we don't always, at least not all of us, take full advantage of that, gay men more than anybody have the innate ability to do so. Some just don't because even though we can be proud to be gay and are mostly unashamed about it, we still have to face the pressures from society of looking and being what the idea of the standard of a "man" is supposed to be. After all, who wants to be called "Faggot" on the bus at one in the morning, or have a car hurl a glass beer bottle at us while we're walking down the street? Depending on where you grew up and when, this was the reality for a lot of us back in the day, especially those of us who grew up in the hood.

I think that this is what enamored me with feminine gay men who I would see carelessly gallivanting about Union Station on Fridays. They were themselves, in their heels with a full goatee, or wearing fitted clothes and slinging hair extensions, and sometimes, dressed like thug trade and sashaying harder than women, talking loud and using gay lingo, sometimes speaking in pig latin. They didn't give a fuck, and that intrigued me, and to this day is why I have such an affinity for gay men who can just be themselves and not give a damn about how anybody else sees them. To me, that's a real man. It takes guts to own your space in the world and be deliberate about doing so. And in a world that follows trends, balks at originality and prides itself much too often on being unkind, it's refreshing to witness that kind of fierceness. Perhaps that's why I admired them so much, being so young and still dealing with church drama, shame, and the reality that back then, my mother still wasn't about to accept having a gay son, it let me know that at the end of the day, I was alright. At least until I was at home, or school and would slip up and do something to raise a red flag about my sexuality, then I'd have to start all over again, and every Friday night would begin the next cycle.

I don't know why, but back then, being clocked by one of the queens was more frightening to me, than when I was being read by my mother for walking around the house with my wrist bent or not speaking with enough base in my voice, or my teammates on our school basketball team, roasting me on the back of the bus on the way to games for being "a faggie". None of that had anything on walking past one of those tables in the food court, downstairs by the movie theater (which is no longer there) and having one of those queens holler out to another one "Oooh, girl look, that's one of our little sisters!" My heart would almost jump out of my chest, I'd swallow hard and try to walk up faster, only to hear them in the distance laughing about how "she is sashaying away as fast as she can, because she got clocked, honey!" I thought they were so evil for that, as I rode up that escalator to the mezzanine level, their cackles piercing through the walkways of the mall. I think that would've scared any semi-closeted gay adolescent, who wasn't quite ready, or didn't know how to come out, although all the signs were clearly there, and nobody knows gay like another gay person, I will always believe that "Family knows Family."

It got even scarier when they'd come where I was and strike up conversations with me. I didn't want to be seen out talking to one "one of them", that would mean that you're one, and you didn't want that getting back to anybody, because once it did, it would always come up that you were out there "playing with faggies." I did get caught a couple of times, talking to flamboyantly gay men in public, and once I knew that I was caught, I'd have anxiety about it, until by some chance one of those queens came face to face with whoever might be teasing me, usually a dude from the school football team or around the way, and hearing one of the queens go "Oh girl, I fucked him last week. He's a big bottom." I would be in awe listening, probably with my chin on the floor as they volunteered full detail "Yes girl, right behind Rhode Island Avenue Metro station. I rolled that football jersey up around his neck and slayed those wombs down, and the whole time, he was singing like Diana Ross!" This was before camera phones and screenshots and all that existed, but those queens would always give you enough information or somehow have enough evidence so that you knew that they were telling the truth. They'd confidently wink at me, pinch my face and assure me "So the next time he messes with you, tell him you know what he did behind Rhode Island Avenue." I never did that, and I'm not much of the type who would spill anybody's tea like that, but after they would see me and a certain queen, especially the two folks who I am referring to in this incident that occurred behind the metro station, things would click and I wouldn't be bothered again.

As hard as I tried to act like I wasn't gay and all that other stuff, they didn't give me any slack, they'd corner me somewhere in the food court, or in the Sam's Club Music Store, B. Dalton books (which were my favorite hang outs in there) and go "Oh child, cut it out and kill the façade. You're in Union Station on a Friday night, browsing through Patti LaBelle and Chaka Khan CD's." They'd snatch me by the arm, and parade me around the mall, through all the spots in DC where the action was, especially 5th & K, which was before DC became so gentrified, where all "the girls hung out at night to take rides and make their coin." A couple of them did sex work, some did that and sold weed, loose cigarettes, did hair or whatever they had to do in order to make money. For a while, I thought that was something that I had to do, not because I needed the money, because I didn't. Back then, I'd just started a part time job at Express. I just thought that it was something that I had to do, just like for a long time, when I'd be downstairs at the library watching men fuck each other in bathroom stalls and stairwells, that that was the way to meet a boyfriend. Until I learned better, I simply just never elected to "find a boyfriend" that way because I wasn't interested in sharing with so many other people.

I can't tell you how many guys I approached in the oddest circumstances to try to see if they'd be interested in going out for a romantic evening somewhere. Those queens, along with my best friend Wayne, were the ones who had to break it to me that the men in those kinds of places practically lived in cruising spots where we'd see them, and probably didn't care for any kind of "romance" outside of those places. Being young and naïve, I didn't understand it, and was still determined to do what I wanted. I never met anyone on that corner, or in the bathroom, but I did meet this boy one night coming out of one of the clubs or glory holes in the old Navy Yard part of town, back when the area was full of nightlife, nightclubs, bars, sex theaters and a couple of other establishments. I think I was just happy to be out and about and have freedom to see men. I met the guy and we had a decent enough conversation outside of whatever club, maybe *The Follies* that we'd met outside of. Never leaving me completely unsupervised, my friends were really bold, if they saw somebody who gave them the wrong vibe, or they knew some stories about, they'd walk up, grab me by my arm and go "Oh no, bitch." Looking back, who knows what kind of trouble they saved me from, and what situations they kept me out of.

There's an expression that says "A hard head makes a soft behind." They figured that I just couldn't quite get it, and loosened their reigns on me a little, and particularly that evening when they let me exchange numbers with this dude. I was given a patient smile and a very calm but loaded "You'll learn." I did. They were right, the guy while he was always nice to me and we never had any falling outs, did bring a lot of drama into my life for that short period of time that he was in it. He almost ruined a friendship, by sleeping with this other sex hungry guy I was friends with, who was older and I befriended because he had his own place and would give me money on a regular basis. I couldn't take guys back to my mom's house, so I would take them there, and behind my back, whoever I'd bring, he'd try to have all of them. Then this dude that I met, moved in with that "friend" of mines, and occupied the room that was supposed to be mines! There was high drama for a while, but eventually, he called himself making nice with me and got back on my good side. That was super easy, because at the time I was hella gullible.

My friends would tell me, "Bitch, you'll learn. We love you, but at this point, we're just here to wipe the snot, tears and dust off of you." The final straw was an STD. I've only experienced that twice in my life, and dealing with him was the first time. We'd never even had sex, he just gave me a blow-job one night, and four days later, I thought my ding-a-ling was about to fall off. I didn't know anything about sexually transmitted diseases. This again is where my friends came in, I called them from a pay phone one night after I got off and explained what was happening, still young and with a lot of innocence I remembered whispering "I think my penis caught a cold." Peaches, whose real name was Darryl, was always tickled by my naivety, would play on it as far as he could, to get as many laughs out of it, while almost giving me an anxiety spasm. He responded "Well the weather is changing, and that can happen if you're walking around in the cold with your fly open." I started listening concerned and trying to figure out where to get Nyquil Cold & Flu for my private parts. "Well what has it been doing? Has it been coughing and sneezing and stuff?" I thought about his question, responding again as innocently as I could, "No, it just has like a runny nose, and a lot of mucus and stuff. It's kind of yellow." I could hear him on the other end, probably almost exploding in tears, trying to hold back his laughter. He finally regained his composure and said "Boo, You can't catch colds in your dick. It doesn't have that type of system. You have an STD and you're gonna have to go to a doctor or a clinic." He broke it all down for me, and let me know that it was nothing to be ashamed of—"Nothing to be proud of either, you don't wanna be out here treating it like its Pokemon and trying to catch them all either, but living in a big city and being sexually active in any capacity, it could happen."

I'd learned about HIV and all of that, but learning about STDs was a completely different territory and it made me even more afraid of sexual contact and trying to date. I didn't want any more surprises, and surely, as they'd warned me, I would learn and I did, and although I had a few missteps, like true friends, they were there for me, each time.

Thankfully, it happened right around the time I was 18, and could schedule and go to doctor's appointments by myself. Up until then, my mother scheduled and would sit in the room while the doctor gave me whatever examinations. I snuck and scheduled the appointment and was able to get one a day after, but I was really scared, because I didn't know what to expect when I went in there. Leaving me up to my own imagination, I half way started to believe that the doctor would have to take it off and reattach it. Just because I was a ball of nerves, Peaches got one of his guy friend's cars, and drove it without a license, picked me up and took me to my appointment. In the parking lot, he grabbed my crotch area through my jeans and started hollering an outrageous prayer of healing and speaking in tongues. He was playing, but in his own little way letting me know he was concerned, and trying to cheer me up. After he assured me that I'd be fine, he took some Purell and sanitized the fuck out of his hands. "I know I touched your jeans, but un-uh honey, I don't know what that's giving, you might have a new strain of something." We laughed and he walked me upstairs into the office and everything got taken care of. None of my friends said anything else about it, they just let the experience speak for itself.

From then on, although I did date a few heartbreakers, I became more selective and did a better job of figuring out who I was trying to deal with. For a whole lot of reasons besides the scare, was still afraid of having sex or going too far with anybody. I also allowed my friends, especially my best friend to offer their input on things that I may not know I may be doing. Even now, years later, I don't think that a friends opinion always has to be the be all, end all, but if you are fortunate enough to have good, genuine, sincere friends who really love you and have your best interest at heart, that it never really hurts to see what it is that they have to say. When you have people who really love you, that can be on the outside looking in, it can make all the difference to your sometimes clouded perspective in the world.

I learned quite a few lessons and gained a lot of knowledge from those early friends, and experiences. Most of all, getting to actually know the people who were my brothers, sisters, bristas, helped me to be able to dispel the horrible things that I was being told in church, and sometimes at home about the people who I guess lived under the same labels, had many of the same experiences, helped me get through them and despite what society said about feminine men, punks, sissies or whatever else they're called, I watched them own their lives fiercely. They nurtured me through a lot of those trying times that many of us were faced with during those early days of coming out, and accepting your sexuality. Over a couple of short years, I lost contact with that crew of folks who saw me, timid and in my shell at Union Station on Friday nights. A couple moved away, one to Texas, another to Louisiana, a couple I'd run into occasionally during a night out, and we'd embrace and start talking, picking up right where we left off. "Is your dick still catching colds?" "I see you're not still putting that artificial base in your voice anymore. Look who's completely out of the closet." It's always fun to see them, now in their late 30's and early 40's and still just as vibrant, sassy and over the top and looking better than ever—you know black don't crack. I really think that most gays age well, it's a requirement, especially since we measure age differently. After you turn 30, you're old, time to sign up for GAYAARP.

A couple of the others passed and maybe another handful, I would love to know where they are in the world. Although they were in mines for such a short period, having them find me and scoop me up from those Friday nights at Union Station and be a part of my life at such an important time where I was affirmed and assured that I could be me and accept myself, and were there during times that could have turned out differently for me, were GOD sends. Eventually, I befriended a new little crew of guys, there were 5 of us, and we all had our own personalities and would go at it, but I couldn't have asked for a better bunch. We are all grown now too, of course. I still have my same best friend. Having them, all these little gay boys, who were just like me, but somehow had more freedom than I, that I kind of envied, but loved to see them make work, by calling my mother and helping her come to terms with my sexuality, and accept me, and Lord knows they'd go at it. It was a blessing, having them encourage me to develop a sense of fashion, and learn how to throw shade, put pomp in my step, not settle for just any type of dude, and most of all, be the very best black queen

I could be was something that in a lot of ways I feel, saved my life and me a lot of trouble, gave me so many awesome experiences and memories. I'm so glad that those were the times I got to experience coming out, and the fierceness of and the love that does exist in this community, and to think, for me, it all started on Friday nights at Union Station, and on the streets of DC.

4. Attack of the
Closeted Church Queens

I grew up Pentecostal Apostolic, where the saints proclaimed to be wrapped up, tied up, tangled up in Jesus, washed in the blood of Christ, and fire-baptized. They took the Bible literally and summed up their beliefs as "God said it, I believe it, and that settles it." Everything was about holiness. I spent many Sundays in that church listening to the pastor stand in the pulpit and rattle off a list of things off that could get you tossed into the lake of fire for eternity. Among the long list of "sins," which seemed to fault people, simply for being human, was the greatest of sins, and one that was unforgivable: being a homosexual.

I had no idea that I was one of the people he was referring to until one Sunday afternoon, during Elder Smith's overly dramatic altar call, with the air stuffy and a broken air conditioner offering no relief from the July humidity. Elder Smith leaned forward over the congregation, tall and mighty from his pulpit, taking inventory of his exhausted but still very engaged congregation, as he bellowed, "I know it's hot in here, and the air would be fixed if more of the saints paid their tithes and offerings...but if you think it's hot in here, then you really gon' be fanning your butt in hell!"

He would reference a "sin" and attach a Bible verse to it, while reminding the congregation that hell was much hotter. We had the chance to claim our salvation while the heat was at least bearable. I remember looking around hoping that folks would take him up on his offer so that they could join the rest of us in heaven, until the pastor lashed out, saying, "And nobody will have a hotter seat in the lake of fire than these nasty, sick, perverted homosexuals. You're a boy, you don't have no business kissing no boys!" That's when it hit me like a ton of bricks: Oh, shit. He's talking about me. Oh, my God, I'm a homosexual.

I was about 13 years old, and I'd never done much sexually, but I knew something was different about me. I couldn't quite put a finger on what it was, but that thing I knew was different about me made me think about kissing and behaving affectionately towards other boys. I felt ice in my fingertips and stood; my mother tapped my shoulder and nodded toward the pulpit. I remember feeling a certain guilt and shame as I took what seemed like a mile-long journey up to get the "gay demons" prayed off of me. After all, I didn't want to disappoint Jesus and definitely didn't want to go to hell.

I'll never forget that pastor, looking at me as if he were staring at Satan face to face while he slung blessed oil in my direction saying he could see the homosexual spirits on me. A series of prayers were issued over me, and the pastor proclaimed that when I left the altar I'd be healed of homosexuality. During the walk back from the altar, I made eye contact with a very attractive junior deacon and felt the wave of heat and excitement wash over me that always did when I saw an attractive male. I figured that the healing hadn't kicked in, and I managed not to feel guilty. I was torn for years, knowing I was being gay while praying for and expecting deliverance, until a series of events occurred that assured me I was OK and, most of all, the Lord definitely worked in mysterious ways. Of all those incidents, the most revealing was taking a trip to get an HIV test, where I ran into the pastor coming in for a test as I was leaving.

After sitting there and listening to him preach fire and damnation against folks for not only having sex before marriage but also being gay, seeing him stroll into Whitman-Walker Clinic (which caters primarily to LGBT people in the D.C. area) was telling. We made eye contact, but of course he made sure to avoid a conversation by never coming close enough to me to say anything — but what needed to happen happened, and the truth was revealed. From that day on, I developed an awareness of not only church hypocrisy in general but the fact that you can't choose who you are attracted to, and that not all pastors practice what they preach despite encouraging their congregations to "give up ways of the flesh."

Perhaps these are some of my biggest contentions with pastors like Bishop Eddie Long and gospel singer Donnie McClurkin. Long, the pastor of Atlanta's New Birth Missionary Baptist Church, was notorious for his homophobic sermons, where he stood in his pulpit and described gay sex as abominable and that men who used their penises to pleasure other men were violating God's laws. In 2010 he was caught up in a scandal in which a group of young gay men came forward and shared very explicit details of intimate relationships they alleged they'd secretly had with the pastor in exchange for money, vacations, and gifts. The scandal nearly destroyed the church. However, the congregation rallied around the embattled megachurch pastor and swept whatever they could under the rug.

Not long after that, Donnie McClurkin appeared at the 2011 Church of God in Christ convention (which is basically like a black gay pride celebration) and urged the youth who might be struggling with homosexuality to come to the altar and be delivered. In tears, he cried out to the congregation that "the children are being lost and failed by the people in their generation." This was in reference to singer B. Slade, formerly known as Tonex, a gospel singer, who had come out as gay. McClurkin, painting himself as the ex-gay poster child of the black church, issued a rebuke and called being gay a perversion of our youth and the church. McClurkin declared that if it hadn't been for Christ, he himself would still be a homosexual. He even insinuated that young people's sexuality is affected by fatherlessness. I listened to him and rolled my eyes so hard up in my head that I thought they'd be stuck that way. When they finally came back down, I watched in anger as young gay and lesbian people threw themselves on the altar — similarly to how I'd done back when I was in church, praying for Jesus to make me a heterosexual.

The funny thing is, I'd come in contact with two people who'd shown me evidence that this man, although preaching that everyone else should be "delivered," was indulging in some of the same behavior and having the time of his life. A couple of years after that, McClurkin was still making antigay statements that were so awful that he was disinvited from a March on Washington memorial concert in Washington, D.C., in 2013. When the Supreme Court ruled for marriage equality last year, McClurkin issued a statement of disgust and urged his church to "stand against all sin, and not bow [its] knee to it."

Finally, this month, it was announced on TBN, a Christian TV network that McClurkin was engaged to gospel singer Nicole C. Mullen. Almost as soon as that statement was issued, it was retracted, and several gospel outlets apologized for sharing the information. Donnie released a video explaining that the couple needed more counseling before trying to move forward. I wonder why?

I'm bothered by all of the scenarios that I've laid out. First, that there are still women who would marry or even entertain the thought of marrying a gay man, especially a gay man who's turned his self-hatred into a war on LGBT congregants and believers. It bothers me having friends who are very aware of their homosexuality pray for a cure while either abstaining or sneaking around and having sex, indulging in what's genuinely natural to them, and feeling unloved by God. It bothers me that there are those who are fine with being LGBT and in relationships but still attend churches that bash gay, lesbian, bisexual, and trans people, staying because the music is good or they don't want to attend a "gay" or affirming church because it's too different. That's like being in an abusive relationship where the motherfucker whoops your ass every week, but you stay because he makes good waffles and the sex is good. Honey, trust me, you can do better. I took my three LGBT dollars out of the tithe basket and walked out of that church a long time ago. I'm more emotionally and spiritually healthy because of it.

There are so many horrifying stories, like Andrew Chad Caldwell, who in 2014 proclaimed that he was "delivert" and he would no longer carry a purse, wear makeup, date men, or wear a bright yellow, frilly bow tie (shocker: he still digs men). Seeing our impressionable youth forced to suppress their sexuality saddens me. Many of these youth live in self-loathing and fear, isolation and terror, while these pastors and gospel singers go to these hotels and sex parties — sometimes held during church conventions — and indulge in the same behaviors. I think about the men who came out against Eddie Long and the pastor I saw when I was leaving from getting tested that day and the fact that any church you go to on a Sunday morning is full of gay men. We are pillars of our communities inside the church and out, while in many religious communities we face a "don't ask, don't tell" policy, and hypocritical behaviors are overlooked. I wonder what is it going to take for everybody to live in truth and all of us to simply be free?

5. *Prisoner of My Own Mind*

I've dealt with depression off and on for most of my life. It's not something that I really talk about—when has that ever been a fun conversation to have? It can be extremely uncomfortable, opening up and making yourself as vulnerable as you do when you share that about yourself with someone. I have a couple of really close friends who know and have seen me sometimes struggle with it, while other times, I kick it's butt. Then, there are those moments where depression has left me flat on my back, in bed, completely devoid of hope, enthusiasm or able to create or accept any solutions, or see any light at the end of the tunnel. I often use to joke when my friends would call or text me, trying to encourage me to cheer up, saying "Everything is going to be alright. Just look for the light at the end of the tunnel." I'd always say "Well muthafucka, I'm suicidal. What the fuck do you think I'm trying to do? Of course, I'm getting ready to go look for it."

The most difficult part is that when you can also spend so much time being the life of the party, joking, turning up and always having a great sense of humor, and appearing happy, while others can sometimes forget that you're a person, with feelings and emotions, and that you have to confront pain in your life, just like everybody else. As human beings, we all do of course, and I think that that's a thing so many people fail to realize, that's why we see people with money, sometimes millions of dollars even, and homes, cars, popularity, careers and lifestyles that other people envy, still unhappy and living with pain and in darkness. They still succumb to depression and the burden that simply living can sometimes be, and being trapped sometimes alone in the absolute torment that living in one's own mind can be, and elect out of this existence. I know so many who have, who've been on the brink, and Lord knows, more than once, I've been on the brink as well.

We become isolated and wake up every day in this unimaginable mental pain. It's kind of like breaking a bone, or straining a muscle, and constantly taking painkillers that put you to sleep, and while you're sleep, the effectiveness wears off, and you wake up, and the first wrong move, you feel that deep, dull, nagging pain that just won't go away and don't seem to heal. Except in life, our pain killers can be much different, alcohol, sex, excessive shopping, junk food, drugs, anything to help soothe that pain, and once that high is over, that nagging pain that haunts you starts all over again. To complicate matters, sometimes people who know you won't, maybe they just forget, to take the time to stop, look at you and acknowledge you as a person. I've felt like that, that my mom may forget that I'm Sampson, a person, with feelings, who faces challenges in life, things that are difficult, and goes through things that cause me to feel a little anti-social at times. I live across the country from her, which of course, some parents do have a really hard time with that and for instance, mines will assume that because I've cut my phone off, or won't return calls right away that I'm "being grown" and ignoring the calls. I'm only looked at as "son" and as soon as we talk, I'll get ripped into, when sometimes you just need to be observed as a person.

Sometimes, it's nice to just have someone, especially if they are close to you, just call and ask "How are you? You've been a bit distant lately and I want you to know that I love you and just wanted to make sure that everything is going ok." Then, there are other times, I have friends who just assume that I am being anti-social and want to know "Why you're being a bitch?", while sometimes it's awesome to get that call, and the remedy for a slump that you've fallen into can be a fun night out of dancing, cocktails, laughing and passing a joint around in a car, being carefree, other times, we fall into pits that are a lot deeper, darker and harder to climb out of. I feel like being in those pits, and having people do the wrong things, respond to you in the wrong ways, and of course fighting the battle of depression alone, without whatever proper help that you need simply buries you. You aren't able to claw your way out, and it simply smothers you to death.

Even as I've sat here, writing about the topic, I've had to acknowledge to myself, just how hard even thinking about, or sharing the reality of depression, and having suicidal thoughts is. I feel like on an even drastically deeper level for people of color, because in a lot of ways, we've been taught throughout our existence in this country, that we don't have feelings, and no matter where we are or what it is that we are responding to that we don't have a right to feel the way that we feel. If it's filling out job applications that we can't seem to get callbacks on, that we're doing something wrong, and need to pull ourselves up by our bootstraps. While we constantly see black youth murdered by those sworn to protect us, that we can't get in the streets and turn out the city halls in protest, it's obvious we were doing something wrong, and that's what happens when you break the law, or a police officer finds you threatening, that they just get to kill you with no repercussion. Our families caution us to not talk about being raped or molested by an aunt or uncle, and going to those family reunions and have everyone act like there is nothing that happened, or something like being told that to be a man means you can't cry, you can't or shouldn't show emotion, among so many other examples that I could list here, have in a way taught us that how we feel doesn't matter, and that if we do having a feeling about something that could bring shame or "stir the pot" that we should suppress those feelings. We've been trained to believe that, so why on earth would we acknowledge depression? And to mention suicide is completely out of the question because "that's not something that black people do.", which couldn't be further from the truth.

For a lot of us, being fucked up in the head is just another day, we're taught that we have to carry the weight of the world on top of our heads, and that that's just how it is, that we can't trust anybody. A lot of us are intelligent enough to "call a thing a thing", and are able to acknowledge that we're depressed, but because of the hustle of life, aren't able to stop and deal with it. I was having a conversation with a friend about depression, grieving, being stressed out, feeling pushed to your limit, and we both stopped to make an observation, "You ever notice that people who have to work every day can't afford to have nervous breakdowns?". If we do, who's gonna pay that expensive ass AT&T bill, rent, and electric while we're busy panicking and not able to function? So, we self-medicate, by hitting up a liquor store, or our weed man, stop past Popeyes, a Chinese carry out, Dominoes, a grocery store for a tub of Haagen Daaz and deal with it that way. Of course, doing that over time, can lead to greater problems.

Stress, which is a killer alone can add to anxiety, elevated blood pressure, etc. While we pile on other things to help it out, foods high in fat, hard liquor, and other unhealthy alternatives to dealing with our issues, and end up with health problems that kill us prematurely. So, whether we go jump off a cliff or not, ultimately, we're still committing a form of suicide, the latter is just a slower, more comfortable way out. Other people may avoid that, and simply elect to constantly go to church and just pray. That's the only thing, pray, pray, pray, pray and if they still see no changes, pray some more, and while I am a firm believer in GOD, and the power of prayer and faith, I'm also a believer that GOD is a GOD of common sense. Let's face it, there are some things that you simply cannot pray away. I believe that you may be able to pray for the strength to deal with those things, but ultimately, as a human being, you need to be helped on a real human level. How do you do that when we live in a society that simply encourages us to "push through" and not deal with real human issues?

A very important part of self-care involves us going to a doctor or a therapist to be acknowledged on a human level. This isn't always easy either, because depending on where you live, your income, medical benefits, you aren't always afforded the privileges of quality healthcare. A lot of what's offered to us is completely subpar, and many of the doctors are out of touch with the needs of their patients. Some haven't taken the time to do thorough research, and I don't mean the type of research where we're treated like science or social experiments, but the kind where people who are educated in medial matters, and are passionate about what they do, take the time to see what the needs of the community are, and how they can reach that community and be effective and going about meeting the needs of the community and seeing what that requires. Some of them simply need to learn what to or not to say out of their mouths, and actually learn to care about creating more positive experiences and making patients comfortable with coming in. It would great to see more of us actually receive care so great that we are enthusiastic about doctor's visits.

I always wonder, how do we acquire good mental health treatment and the hope needed to be proactive to do so, when our doctors can barely hold it together during basic check-ups? During one of my last doctor's visits, I left his office appalled. I hadn't had a check-up in at least five years. Any HIV tests, etc. I had gotten at free clinics, or on testing vans and any ailments that I felt I had, I went for acupuncture or herbal remedies, or something like that. I'd definitely shied away from an actual doctor's office for years, because one, with the exception of the physician I had at 18, they all were careless and didn't give a damn, and because of a lot of healthcare options that I looked at were too expensive, and the waiting lists and hoops that one has to jump through sometimes for Medicare, or government assisted medical insurance was too much to deal with. Thankfully, Obamacare and a couple of other very reasonable options came along, and I was able to finally get some decent health coverage. I had to wait about two months to get an actual appointment, but at least, I was finally able to see a doctor. There was a sense of pride and relief that I had, being able to finally walk into a doctors' office and get a check-up. That is, until I met the doctor, and realized that he didn't know what the hell to say out of his mouth. His first question was "So how healthy do you think you are? You think your lungs and cholesterol are ok? Do you smoke weed and eat a lot of fried chicken and stuff?" I was really *trying* to believe that he wasn't "going there", but as he continued with his questions, I realized that I wasn't trippin'. "What's your family health like? Your mother? What about your dad? Do you know anything about him?" He continued, "What's your sex life like? How many times have you had STDs?" Not "have you ever had", he went directly to "how many times have you had STDs?"

I couldn't believe it, sitting in this doctor's office, watching, and listening to this condescending white man, ask me all of these ridiculous questions, make dumb assumptions, be insensitive about what he was asking, then asked for me to strip down so he could take a look at my dick and balls. He called it a "package", as he chuckled, waving his finger around in the general direction of it. I left that office feeling like a gotdamn science experiment and I'm pretty sure by the time I go in for my next check-up that I'll look for another doctor, even if I do have to travel across town to visit. But think, being treated that way, who would want to go visit a doctor's office, especially if they were expressing issues affecting their thinking and mental, emotional well-being and were met with a barrage of insults, condescending questions, and stupid remarks? With the level of stress, and some of the things that we are forced to deal with on a daily basis, especially as minorities, I wonder how capable many of these medical professionals are at not only dealing with our bodies, but also helping us cope effectively cope with our mental ailments? This makes it harder to simply encourage those in need of it to "get help". How do you get help when "the help" is making the journey to mental wellness and recovery that much more frustrating?

Sadly, the doctor's offices aren't the only places that inflict these harms, many churches which have been known as places to come and be restored, or "hospitals for the broken" can be just as bad. I've never cared much for that expression either, because depending on what's wrong with you, the hospital can be the worst place for you to go, and too many people have gone there and simply died, sometimes because doctors have done all humanly possible to save the life. On the other hand, many people have also died in hospitals because some doctors have not been trained sufficiently enough, and sometime because of malpractice. The latter two have occurred most often in churches, and had I not been smart enough to leave when I did, who knows what other kinds of trauma and pain I would have continued to be forced to live with.

Especially in our culture, faith, GOD, prayer, church, in fact religion itself, are the cornerstones of many people's lives. When many of us have nothing else to hold onto, we hold onto GOD, faith, relationships with spiritual and religious community, which all are definitely important. When I was younger, I loved GOD—still do, and pray daily and often quite fiercely, I didn't understand, but as I've gotten older and gone through life, I've come to understand that none of us can do it on our own. We need to be able to lean on the power of something far greater than we are, and again, I certainly do. Being able to rest on the power of something greater is important to me, when I hear people thank GOD for health, wellness and a sound mind, I completely get it, especially with all the mental and emotional challenges that life can yield, I've realized that I am blessed to still be alive, standing and in my right mind.

However, it took me a long time to be able to separate my relationship with a higher force, from the horrible relationship and experiences that I had with people who called themselves "representatives of GOD." While they labeled me and other folks who dealt with real life human issues that they truly didn't have the love of GOD in their heart to understand, "full of demons". I can't tell you how many times I've been up to an altar and had pastors, with their hot, stank breath blowing in my face, and you know bad breath stinks worse when people "H words", and I endured a lot of hot, funky breath because they just LOVE saying the word "Hell", would look me in my eyes, with a look of absolute disgust and hatred, and address me as "Satan". This happened each time I was forced onto the pulpit or altar for prayer, for being gay, and also for dealing with depression. When I'd reveal to a family member that I was gay or dealing with depression, or both, I'd be shoved and pulled up front and got these "exorcisms" almost weekly.

Part of me wanted to get down on all fours and go running out of church like a hyena, making wild billy goat sounds just to fuck with everybody. But before I learned to walk away, or just not go, I'd stand there with some crazy bimbo in a suit, calling themselves a reverend. They'd push and pull on my forehead making me feel even worse than I did before I came in. The fact that we're constantly told that mental challenges, which are a byproduct of the human condition are not of GOD—who after all created human beings and knows all about us can render a young person, or even a person who simply isn't educated enough to ask questions or separate the bullshit with either a false sense of hope that things will just take care of themselves. Sadly, this leads to horribly unrepressed and unresolved issues that can lead to even greater problems when they go back into the real world from those church doors.

This is a classic example of folks being so heavenly bound that they are of no earthly good and is one of the reasons why even today, I am cautious of a lot of churches and have become far removed from the idea that you can really "pray anything away". That really bothers me that in so many of these important professions and institutions that those who have the power and influence to help those dealing with these serious issues like depression and mental health fail horribly doing so, and while you ultimately do not get to decide whether or not someone will or won't take their own lives, dammit, we have a hell of a lot of impact as fellow human beings. I think that so many people who would still be here today, are not, because of how horribly the reality of mental illness has been swept under the rug or if dealt with, done so daintily and not treated as something that can cripple a person's entire being.

It takes a lot to get up every day while dealing with something that intense, pull your face up as best you can, get dressed and go out into the world. Maybe because I've had so many friends who I watched battle it, or because I know the sting of depression and the darkness that it brings into your life, the cloud that hangs over your head, no matter what you try to do, or how you try to shake it, that I am very cognizant of how I treat people when I interact with them. There's even an expression that simply says "Be kind, you never know the battles that another person may be fighting", and a little bit of kindness can go a very long way. In fact, you could be someone's reason to keep fighting and with the right support, not just fight, but win. Despite the intense dark places that I've landed in those times when I did fall into depression, with the grace of GOD, and support, or light, even if I didn't always know where it was going to come from, or if I'd simply have a moment where I could have enough enlightenment to snap out of my trance, I got it. For a long time, I didn't think black people got depressed, or got to have emotions other than "tired" or "on the way back to that damn job.", maybe even happy or sad, but no complexity of emotion in between. When it came to being depressed, I was always taught that that wasn't something that black folks went through. Hell, there were a lot of things that I didn't know black folks had I didn't know that we had estrogen and testosterone levels, I thought that those were white people things, and I think again that the fact that many of us aren't aware of the changes that our mental health my face, let alone our bodies proves that we almost have to live up to a kind of super human idea of ourselves, although we are human just like anyone else of any other race or national background.

My most recent bout dealing with depression mirrored that exact theory. I've always been looked at as a warrior, a champion and have always felt constantly pressured to live up to that, even when I was growing up. My father left when I was a young baby, and aside from the two long term male partners that my mother had, I was the man of the house, and even when those relationships ended and my mom and I became homeless for a few years, I still had to assume that responsibility. Perhaps that's why my work ethic is so strong now, because I didn't spend many Saturdays in in front of the television, eating Fruit Loops, watching cartoons. We were up at 630 or 7AM, packing vacuums, cleaning supplies and buckets into the trunk of my mom's 1989 Geo Storm, so that we could go clean houses and offices all day. That's the way that we made the money to afford a hotel to stay in, and storage to place excess clothes, belongings and cleaning supplies. We did that for years, on weekends, and when I'd get out of school, my mom would come and pick me up and take me back to come filthy apartment that she'd spent scrubbing floors and toilets at all day. I'd help her finish it, and by 9 o'clock that night, we'd get to head in. Every now and then, things would slow down and she wouldn't be able to find a place to clean, so we'd have to sleep in that car, cramped up and close to penniless. Those days and nights when the weather rendered extreme heat or frigid temperatures, made it even more challenging.

I also still managed to get fairly decent grades in school, and my mom still put many of the expectations that some of our parents place upon their young boys. Maybe because we'd gone through so much together, so much, even things that I'm remembering that I am not writing, they were rough times, and I know that she looked to me for a source of inspiration to help us continue through those hardships. But it seemed like she'd be kind of disappointed of I was tired, or just couldn't jump in a deep pool and swim in it, or fix something, or got into a fight that I couldn't win (which happened a couple of times before I learned how to fight, growing up) and in a lot of ways, because I knew she depended so much on me, even if I had to scrape my very soul to pull something off, I'd push myself to my absolute limits. I was doing this around 10 and 11 years old. I'm sure that as a single mother trying to make ends meet without any help equally pushed her to many limits as well. I think it's really crazy that so many minority youth don't get to fully enjoy our childhoods because we face so many stressful situations that push us into emotions and frustrations that because of circumstance, we don't have the luxury of getting to take any time to deal with them, or have things like family dinners where we can talk about how we feel, or things that may be bothering us.

It was such a surprise when I got my first white friend, Richard Brown, who we nicknamed "Cornbread" in middle school. We called him that because even though he was white, the boy was black. He could dance, had rhythm, and loved soul food. We got a total kick out of him. He took me to visit a cousin of his, who didn't get the soul, rhythm and swag that he did. The cousin of his that we went to visit was just a pure, white bread cousin and family who lived out in the suburbs. One night, during dinner, I watched Richard's cousin cuss out both of his parents and insult the size of his dad's penis. I sat there in awe because I'd never seen anything like that before. Although it was out of pocket (inappropriate, out of control) I watched this kid express disdain, emotion and it never occurred to me that that was just what it was. While a child cussing out their parents rightfully does deserve to have their mouth rinsed out with soap, and probably yanked up in their collar, I think now, looking back, it is important for youth to be able to respectfully be able to say "I don't like this.", "This is hard for me.", "This hurts." Sometimes, it's not easy to just push past the hurt and emotions because they simply remain dormant and unresolved and it's something that we never have learned to put into practice, particularly as children. We face high levels of stress early and are forced to just deal with it.

This happened to me when I discovered that some folks thought that my dark brown skin and pronounced features were unattractive, when we were homeless, when I was dealing with the whole coming out process, religion and family acceptance drama, and lastly as an adult when I moved across country away from family, friends, and so much of what I'd known all my life, and quit a job that was making me miserable to really focus on my life, and my career in entertainment, and as a stand-up comedian, which by then I'd been doing for well over 10 years. I was use to some of the challenges that came along with show business, especially as an openly gay black man, which brings its own set of issues in this business, and was beginning to face life without the feeling of stability that a bi-weekly paycheck can provide. I was doing this mostly alone, looking for gigs and doing what I needed to do to keep my head above water. I was adjusting to being in a new place where not as many people knew me, that meant that although I had a lot of credentials I needed to have to still work at a similar capacity as a headliner as I was used to, that I did have to in a way start over again. I was also fresh across the country and I had a few friends, but it wasn't as easy to call up my group of buddies like back at home and go "Hey, let's meet up for drinks or food tonight, or go somewhere and get some shit started." I missed that, and I never realized how important good, solid, dependable and trustworthy friendship is, honestly until I felt like I didn't have it at my fingertips or nearby. We all need someone who is dependable, I feel like having that offers a very important all around reinforcement.

Another huge challenge itself, is being a working adult and not having the time to stop to take care of ourselves, it seems like it's impossible to do, but it's definitely something that we need to make sure that we find the time to administer adequate self-care. We get so busy hustling to make sure that we have that next rent or phone bill payment, and for those of us who have kids, that's an entirely different priority that life becomes too hectic to find time to make new friends and build relationships with them, and being a person who is very consumed by their profession, working to make sure that gigs are booked, contracts are signed and returned, answering calls and emails, running errands, catching flights and preparing for shows without much help, when I finally get a moment to look up and breathe, and turn to talk, sometimes there is no one there. In my case, I had a couple of people, but they were just as busy as I was, and then some folks who are close to you, just don't get the big picture. People see you working, turning your wheels, performing at this or that place, posting "fancy" pictures on social media (which isn't a reality, only a snapshot of your life), and assume that you're making lots of money, and after every show retire somewhere into a lap of luxury and that you're somewhere off being fabulous. Very few people realize what a hustle and how much of you, you neglect in order to be on a stage or entertaining folks every night, especially if you don't have a strong support system around you. I had a conversation backstage after a show one night with disco legend Gloria Gaynor, who told me to "never say or look at it as a sacrifice, because that implies regret." I will say there's a lot of pressure, and dealing with that, along with the rejection that minorities face in this business, an even greater level if you have to be a double or triple minority, life itself sometimes, and dealing with constant challenges without a lot of help, led me into one of the deepest depressions that I'd faced in years, like since my late teens.

I think that we all kind of fall into slumps and feel blah, or little periods where we just can't seem to escape the clouds that are hanging over our heads, but this was an even deeper hole. Sometimes, you just can't climb out alone. Every now and then we all need somebody to help us out. I believe in prayer and meditation, but we also require love and care on a human, emotional and psychological level as well. I drifted along silently, in pain, determined to win this battle alone, and it just seemed like nothing would go right, and that anything that could go wrong, did. I began to self-medicate every day, drinking liquor and smoking, to a point where I probably couldn't tell you my name, but still managed to be functional on a day to day basis. As this occurred over the span of a couple months, still trying to keep up with life, and still feeling unsupported, the thoughts that maybe I couldn't do this, and that I couldn't live anymore began to flicker across my thoughts. I fell into an even deeper pit because I started to feel sorry for myself, something that I absolutely loathe! I've never been a thrower of pity parties, but here I was. The thing about getting to a point like that is you can actually feel yourself drifting away and you feel almost helpless in doing anything about it. I felt like I had very few people to lean on, who could understand that I was tired of "being strong" and being the one that everyone else felt should be saving them. I wasn't superman, I was tired, had barely any work, or places to perform, which is one major way that I use to express myself and on top of that, I barely had income. Lord knows, being without a coin is the ultimate putdown.

When you get into a state of depression that intense, you cut yourself off from people, which is what I did. Why should you talk to people if they aren't going to understand? Finally, I made up in my mind that I was ready to elect out of this existence. Life had become way too difficult to navigate. You do think about the people in your life, "What are they gonna do if I do this?" and I simply made peace with my conclusion that everybody would be okay in a couple years and be able to move on with their lives. I was happy with that and that was the plan.

One morning, I got up out of bed, showered, got dressed and went out, caught the train, ended up in San Francisco and just started walking, pretty aimlessly. I zoned out, and before I knew it, I'd walked maybe 10 miles and found myself standing on the Golden Gate Bridge. I could see all across the Bay Area, the Pacific Ocean crashing back and forth looked almost welcoming. The waves rolled and turned, as to assure me that they'd carry me way from my sadness, problems, loneliness, being overwhelmed, rejected, tired, feeling powerless, worthless, even feeling like a failure. Not much else mattered at that moment to me, as I gripped the guard rail and stepped up, starting to muster up the courage to go through with it. Tears welled up in my eyes, my heart began to thump and I felt torn. Alot of thoughts ran through my mind. I thought about Robin Williams, who I'd met and had come to a show that I did one night. He'd passed by now, but I remembered him sitting backstage with me, talking about life, comedy and just shooting the shit. I'll never forget among the many things that he told me, "Not to give up." My brain had lots of other questions, and just as it was racing, I thought about my mother and a couple of my friends who I really love--but alot about my mom, who, although we have our moments where we disagree and go back and forth, that if I did that, that would be a scar on her soul that she would never recover from. That would probably be the worst thing that I could do, not just to her, but the many people who although I don't always feel it, or think it, do love and care about me. I was so frustrated I had no idea what else I could do. I felt trapped with no answers.

Begrudgingly, I backed away from the railing and proceeded down the bridge path in tears. I didn't know what I would do or how things would work out, but it was then, that I decided if I'm going to be here, things would have to get better. They'd need to improve, and mostly that I could not continue to live wallowing in the bottom of the barrel like I had been for those last few months. For a few days, I couldn't do anything but cry. You see, I'm not much of a cry baby, and I'd always learned that in order to survive that I had to put what I was feeling aside, and deal with life as best I could. Yeah, it makes you think you're invincible, but when you finally do feel, you explode, and Lord knows, I had my moments when I'd explode. A few mornings, I woke up angry and would get up out of bed, throwing lamps across the room, turning things over and a few other things that would've put my security deposit in jeopardy when I moved out of my apartment.

Eventually I had to pull the reigns in on things and decide that it was fine to be where I was, as long as I didn't stay there. I love weed, but I had to leave it alone, because if you smoke it too often, yeah, you'll feel good, food will taste great, you can tolerate life and people better, but it can and will derail you. I stopped drinking and put my head back into my work however I could, I started praying and meditating more, and eventually got health insurance and was able to see a doctor who helped me identify my depression and anxiety and agreed that it's always good when you realize that you have an issue like that, that's hindering you from living as good and productive as you are able, and that minorities especially are impacted by the reality of post-traumatic stress, anxiety and bipolar disorder because of the stress that we confront on a daily basis simply because of who we are. It's more expensive to have a nervous breakdown than it is to stop working for a few days or take a vacation. We rarely are able to afford any of those options, so we deal with it, and as a result, usually aren't aware of the consequences until we hurt ourselves. In addition to suicide or self-harm, developing hypertension etc. which are byproducts of stress, or until we hurt someone else. There are too many ways to list here how we do that, or are able to.

I realize how blessed I am to had not made that decision that day. Of course, the thoughts and pain of self-harm didn't just disappear, but I was able to make up to face them head on and sought out the help that I needed and began to challenge myself to do whatever I could to turn things back around. A part of that process involved me making myself be okay with being uncomfortable and realizing that I had to climb back up. I was also able to realize that I did have some people around me who were friends, even associates who cared and offered listening ears and encouragement. Sometimes, you just need someone else to assure you that everything is going to be okay, particularly in times of serious inner turmoil. I also made sure to find time to do things like yoga, which I use to tease folks for because I thought that that was just an activity was white women. I take vitamins and am sure to affirm myself positively every day. If I do feel a little cloud start to come over my head, I'm able to realize that I need to pick up the phone and call or text someone who'll be understanding and empathic, while holding me accountable for finding an effective solution to deal with whatever issue that I'm having.

This definitely yields true that suicide is a long term solution for a temporary issue, and no matter how long temporary issues seem, it's alot less time than it would be, not being here to experience your full potential and eventually find a way to turn things around. Some of us wake up and on a daily basis, have to put on a mask to wear out in the world, pretending that everything is okay, even when life seems to be stagnant and in the shitter. Again, we cope with these things either passively, in silence, and some of us go into the world more radically, ready to take our frustrations out on "the first muthafucka who would." I've done both, and neither is the answer. We never know the battles that one another faces in life, and some, in our heads, especially our brothers and sisters who live everyday battling severe mental illnesses in whatever capacity they may be forced to deal with them in.

It takes a very strong person to realize a mental issue in any capacity, stand up and do what they need to do to address it. That may involve talking it through with a loved one, visiting a healthcare professional, utilizing therapy and taking meds, removing ourselves from stressful situations and focusing on rising to the challenge of finding a healthy solution. Many of us at one time or another have experienced being what feels like a prisoner in our own mind. We just have to realize that for every prison, there's a key, and we don't have to force ourselves to find that key to freedom and wellness alone, or in silence.

6. The Week Baltimore Burned

I sat in front of the television, depressed, hurt, outraged at the fact that yet another black man, Freddie Gray had been murdered by the police. We had already endured the tragedies of Trayvon Martin, Eric Garner and many other black men and women who'd been senselessly gunned down by the police. While I watched the news reports, I totally agreed with the righteous indignation occurring on my screen, while at odds with quite a few friends who don't understand why I supported the uprising, the protest, the anger in Baltimore. Friends sometimes disagree, and that's ok. And other times, people just don't get it. I don't get what's so hard to understand. I've had to break it down as honestly and from as many personal points as I can.

I'm a black, gay man from the South (North Carolina). I grew up in Washington, DC (Baltimore is an extension of DC) and I even lived in Baltimore at one time, as an adult (on 33rd & Greenmont). As a child, I grew up in extreme poverty, we were homeless, on the street for years (since I was 11), sleeping at metro bus stops, in parks, at greyhound stations and hospital waiting rooms. I make jokes about growing up homeless all the time, but it's very painful to take a serious look back and try to make sense out of any of it. We simply needed a helping hand (and tried assistance from shelters and government assistance programs) but any serious efforts made by my mother to improve our situations seemed to come with penalties, and all we needed was a little help, to connect a few dots and pull ourselves out of the hole. We couldn't have both, and to this day, I still believe it had to be a combination of luck, magic and GOD that got us out of that situation, finally when I was 16.

We didn't get a chance to have "emotions". Fighters don't get to cry. And surely, that breeds mental health concerns. What else happens when simply fighting to survive becomes a burden so great that you don't have the privilege of coping with your emotions? I grew up fighting, and I still fight, like a dog for everything that I get. Nothing has EVER been simply dropped into my lap. I've always been a creative. I had to use that and humor to deal with the bullshit that I, and many other kids who I grew up went through. And I watched my mother deal with that whole system of oppression, the entire time that I grew up and was robbed of my childhood because of it. I don't have many fuzzy, warm childhood memories.

On my own journey to making a life for myself, a generation later, I'm no longer homeless, thank GOD, but I still deal with bullshit. Anyone who knows anything about me, knows, that of course, performing comedy is my life. But as with any corporate structure, of course I'm constantly facing ridiculous odds, especially as a comic who happens to be a black male, and gay. I'm DAMN GOOD at what I do, I work hard and make the necessary sacrifices that I need to make in order to be successful and have consistency and still often meet blatant rejection. Agents refuse to pick me up (dozens have told me that I'm not worth the investment and a hard sell), comedy club bookers don't hire me (don't think I'm commercial enough) and I haven't been on television in years (not mainstream enough) and I've been rejected from EVERY SINGLE major comedy or film festival that I've tried to get into, and this has been occurring for over a decade. One morning, I woke in bed, and it all hit me. I woke and snapped, went through my room in a rage, knocking things over, tearing up lamps, broke a few things. If it hadn't had been my belongings I damaged, it would've been myself. I fell on my bedroom floor sobbing hysterically. Tormented by the fact that although I work hard and exceed expectations, I still have to fight a fucking system that doesn't think I'm good enough because of who I am and how I express that. And that bothers me sometimes on a motivational level and on an emotional level, every day.

Similarly, our brothers and sisters deal with challenges that far exceed the ones that I have as much as it hurts me. At least I had a chance to escape, and experience a life a little better than the one that many people have to live in every day, confined to neighborhoods that are looked at as cages that hold worthless savages. You learn to make feel like home, even in dehumanizing conditions. Where no matter how hard you work, it's not enough. You try to make a better life for yourself and make the most out of a little, and it still never be enough. And constantly having the rug pulled out from under you, by the unfairness of life and a detestable system, that continues to deprive you of opportunities to a good quality of life, be treated fairly, have opportunities, and most of all simply be entitled to live. Why wouldn't you want to burn something symbolic of that down?

7. "Reach Out & Touch
(Somebody's Hand)"

*(from message delivered at Metropolitan Community Church-Rehoboth Beach,
DE—Sept. 2015)*

This world can sometimes be a challenging one to live in, to say the least. Watching the news, and even enduring the hardships in our own lives, I'm sure that many of us have wondered, why life at times can be so cruel and punishing, as many of us deal with it's trials that can include loneliness, loss of loved ones, depression, lack of resources for ourselves, and or our families, hunger, poverty, sickness, racism, homophobia, sexism, fear of one another, violence, war, police brutality and countless other calamities.

As children, those of us who were fortunate enough were allowed to experience the world, and life from a shielded lens, which allowed us a more jovial perspective. For a long time, my only care in the world was to make sure that the brownies came out right in my EZ Bake oven. As we got a little older, and our parents realized that we wouldn't always be under their protective eye, they warned us of things to do and what to be aware of, "Don't talk to strangers.", "Look both ways before you cross the street.", "Always wear clean drawls, just in case you end up in an ambulance." Being a young, black male, aging into adolescence, the instructions became more serious, "Make sure you're in the house before the street lights come on.", "Always hold on to your receipts when you leave a store, in case they accuse you of stealing.", "If the COPS pull you over or stop you, keep your hands in sight, do what they say, and respond to them by saying "Yes, Sir", and "No, Sir"." My mother and my elders were aware of the potential hazards that could sometimes exist in our simple day to day living.

Upon migrating to the urban inner city from the south, I became exposed to the realities that I needed to navigate my way through, drive by shootings, robberies, dilapidated school houses and insufficient educational opportunities, poverty, extreme poverty that contributed to elevated levels of crime, drug abuse, hopelessness, misery and despair. I always believed that it was impossible for young people to die. I was forced to reckon with a different reality, seeing kids my age, 12 years old, dead at the hands of police officers or stray bullets. Every morning, before I left for school, or in the evenings to go to a friend's house to play Nintendo, or to go to the playground, a flicker of worry showed in my mother's eyes, as caution filled her instruction to "Please be careful, and make it back home safely."

It didn't take me long to understand that my mother was trying to prepare me for the realities of the world around me. As I grew older, being able to understand the news, I'd hear my elders constantly remind each other that "We were living in our last days." That always scared the hell out of me, because I never knew what that meant. And I always thought that they were lucky, because as old as they were, they would get the benefit of dying peacefully before the world exploded or something, whatever "the last days" meant. For a long time, because I never knew what that meant, I lived in a bubble of fear. It wasn't until after a few epiphanies that I was finally able to break free of the fear of living. Most of all that they aren't "the last days", because life begins where we make up our minds to create it for ourselves and one another. I do believe that somewhere along the way, we've lost our grips on love, humanity, unity, compassion. But that someway, somehow, through doing the work of love, and letting that light that our creator has placed in each of us to shine, that we can find a way to make this world a better place.

My approach to spirituality and religion happen to be a bit unconventional. I'm more than convinced that GOD can speak to us anywhere, through anything or anybody. Some of the best "church" that I've had, has been while eating a piece of hot, crispy fried chicken, because Lord knows, a good chicken wing can minister to your spirit and your soul, I've also found "church", in twirling at an all-night dance party, there's a certain freedom in simply letting go, of all inhibitions, and throwing your troubles to the vibration of a classic house track. In the same way, some of the best sermons that I've heard have come from small children, one being a 7-year-old, who suggested that "If you want to learn to love better, start by loving a friend that you hate.", or my favorite Aunt Jackie, who, while shoving a cigarette into the corner of her mouth, and lighting it, will remind me that "Baby, ain't no use in trying to rush through life, because no matter where you go, there you are!" These statements are simple, yet profound, and with that, I hope that you can be encouraged by "The Gospel of Diana Ross". When it comes to Miss Diana Ross, among the first adjectives to come to mind, is surely "diva". Known as much for her big hair, boas, and immaculate gowns as her ego, there's no denying that Miss Ross is absolutely FABULOUS, honey!

In April 1970, Miss Ross made her departure from her background singers, better known as "The Supremes". As she embarked on her solo career, she recorded a song entitled "Reach out & Touch (Somebody's Hand). This three minute record carried heavy gospel influences and expressed a message meant to invigorate social consciousness regarding the state of the human condition. The chorus of the song is to: Reach out and touch somebody's hand/Make this world a better place if you can/Reach out and touch somebody's hand/Make this world a better place if you can.

I'm here to pose the question to you family, when is the last time you've taken a moment to reach out and touch somebody? Walking down the street and seeing people consumed by iPhones, or the way we avoid eye contact with one another, or simply sometimes failing to return a head nod, hello or a smile, it's quite easy to realize how disconnected we are from one another and how much further we continue to push one another away.

Observing the news of never ending wars, and our children and young adults killed on the streets without justice, as heartless law officials and politicians continue sitting in office as affected communities cry out in protest, I pose the question, when are we going to reach out and touch each other, ya'll? Will it come to a point where we face a collapse as a people so devastating, that the only choice we have is to finally realize that we are in fact one people, who all need each other? As we've become a more self-serving society, we can sometimes look at things and ask, "If this can't benefit me, then why should I care?". I myself am guilty of this type of mentality at times, especially when it comes to those I don't like (conservatives, bigots, people who don't use their turn signals when they're driving in front of me). To selflessly display authentic compassion and loving-kindness, especially when it's not convenient, can be a challenge.

When I'm faced with these kinds of challenges where it's difficult for me to understand the need for love and compassion under all circumstances, I'm often reminded of times in my life when people with their own challenges have failed to extend kindness, love, compassion and understanding to me when I needed it. Among the most difficult of those times were Sundays, sitting in church as a young teenager, aware of my sexuality and listening to the pastor call people like me "Faggots, who were contributing to decline of the structure and masculinity in the black community and an abomination unto GOD, that I was undeserving of human or divine love."

Or, on several occasions, walking down a street, dressed even in nice clothing, but having police officers stop and detain me in handcuffs, on a crowded street of onlookers, because I happened to fit the description of a dark-skinned, black male in jeans, fitted baseball caps and a tee-shirt. I'm reminded of a time, being homeless, sleeping in Greyhound bus stations and a 1989 red, hatchback Geo Storm with my mother in the dead of winter at 14 years old, and often not knowing where food or shelter may come from, ever again. These times have reminded me of what it felt like to be down and in need of a hand.

Then, I'm reminded of the times in those situations, where they became a little easier to deal with and make it through, because somebody reached out to touch me. The times when although she may have been just as hungry, my mother sacrificed a meal to make sure that I ate, while her stomach growled loudly. I think about those nights that strangers allowed us into their homes, and shared their food, allowed us to bathe and sleep on their sofas and floors. Many of these people we never saw again, but helped us out along the way and reminded me that there are people in the world who care.

I was assured of love, when I think about those Sundays, listening to those messages, tears streaming down my face, locking under my chin, because I was being taught that GOD didn't love me, and the woman who'd sit next to me at that church, daring me to put my tithes in that offering plate one Sunday. She pushed my money back into my hands, telling me "GOD loves you baby, and it's not any man's job to try and make anybody believe otherwise." She reminded me of the Nina Simone quote "You have to learn to get up from the table when love is no longer being served." as she grabbed my hand and led me out of that sanctuary. I asked "Oh, you're gay?" and she replied, "No, but I do have a heart."

Having a community of all people, whether they're black, or white, gathering collectively in protest to raise our voices against the arrests of innocent black men in our neighborhoods. Seeing pastors who'd preached damnation to gay, lesbian and transgender people, show up to LGBT events to apologize and learn more about our community, or simply, walking down a street on a day that may be challenging and having a complete stranger smile and tell me "You look nice." or "Have a great day." are all things that have allowed me to reach out and touch somebody else, because somebody touched me. It didn't take anything extreme; all it took was just a touch of love.

In reaching out, many of us may not believe that we have enough to give someone else, because financially, spiritually, emotionally, physically, many of us barely have enough to give ourselves. This makes me think about the backyard parties that we'd have in my little neighborhood growing up. Many of us were poor, sometimes without two pieces of bread to rub together. Nonetheless, we'd decide that we were going to have a big neighborhood party. Piece by piece, we'd bring it all together, one person would bring a pack of hotdogs, somebody else would bring some bread, another person a bag of chips, then some chicken would show up, a little liquor, a boom box, and a box of playing cards. We were broke and didn't have anything, but all of us took our little bit of nothing, brought it to that backyard and made a whole lot of something. We'd end up having some of the best neighborhood BBQ's that you'd ever go to in your life.

In the same way, let's all bring the little bit of what we have to life's big BBQ.

Every day that we are blessed with another opportunity to rise, is another invitation to life's big get together. I challenge us to, on a daily basis ask ourselves "How can I be an expression of love?" Let's go out to life's BBQ and take a few smiles, a little patience, some kind words, and some joy. Let's extend forgiveness, and lift our voices against injustice. GOD's greatest commandment is to love our neighbors as we love ourselves. That means that in this whole process, we must establish self-love that we often forget to give ourselves, because if we can't love ourselves, how can we efficiently love somebody else?

Just touch somebody. If we did this, we could end hunger, and loneliness, depression, and the stigma of HIV. We would eradicate hate crimes, racism, sexism and homophobia. Together, we would thrive and life for all of us could be so much better. Imagine that, a big table for all, where love is the main order, the appetizer, entree and dessert. All we have to do is reach out and touch somebody's hand, make this world a better place if you can. Take a little time out of your busy day, to give encouragement to someone who's lost the way, or would I be talking to a stone, if I asked you to share a problem that's not your own? We can change things if we start giving, why don't you reach out and touch somebody's hand? If you see an old friend on the street and he's down, remember his shoes could fit your feet. Just try a little kindness. You'll see it's something that comes very naturally. We can change things if we start giving. Why don't you reach out and touch somebody's hand, make this world a better place if you can.

8. Funny Is Funny: Homophobia, Misogyny & the Lack of Diversity in Comedy

I'll never forget that hot summer night, sitting in the back of a crowded bar with poor A/C, leaned over the table, reviewing my set list with the light from the muted television mounted against the wall. I was up next and full of my normal preshow jitters. As I stuffed my set list into my pocket, I remember having my train of thought jolted to a sudden holt, by hearing the comic up on the mic scream "What the fuck?! They're gonna give me AIDS through the wall!"

I was so into preparation for my set that I wasn't paying attention to what he was saying before, but that got my attention. He went on for another 10 minutes about his gay neighbors, who he constantly referred to as "butt bandits" and "fags" to the shock and amusement of the crowd and made jokes about how scared he was of catching AIDS through the wall living next to them. I couldn't believe it, I'd heard gay jokes before, and told my own share of crass jokes and bragged about how much pussy I was getting (that's what male comics were supposed to do) but that night, I decided that that couldn't work for me anymore. The emcee introduced me, and as I stepped up to the mic, everything that I'd prepared went out of the window.

Removing the mic from the stand, I remember saying "We've been neighbors all this time, and I have to come to a comedy showcase to find out that's how he feels about living next door to us." The audience chuckled, and from there, I riffed on being gay, how hard life had been for me at the time. By then, I'd been doing comedy for about three years and of course way before then, had been aware of my sexuality. In fact, I was just coming out to my mom, who wasn't taking it too well, going through a horrible break up, dealing with religion and was borderline suicidal. I was at a crossroads in my life, and listening to that idiot triggered a catharsis. My 15 minutes on stage seemed like an eternity, the rant was raw and kind of funny, and I'm sure that the audience definitely felt like they were sitting in on a therapy session, but when I walked off that stage, I finally felt like I'd done something authentic.

I never intended to disclose my sexuality on stage, because to me, it wasn't anyone's business, but doing so allowed me to finally create material from an authentic point of view, which makes the best comedy, or any art for that matter, not to mention, made me as funny as I was off stage, because I could be honest. However, I didn't expect what came next, I was kicked off a small tour that I was on, and lost a weekly hosting gig at a bar because the owner felt like "the patrons wouldn't be able to handle the gay shit." A few nightclubs that I played were particularly hostile, one, where bottles were thrown at me in the parking lot, and another, where a group of guys were waiting outside the club and dared me to "bring that shit back down there."

I persisted however, and continued to develop my authentic voice and was able to use humor to not only talk about life, but do it in a way that all audiences could relate to, and started receiving standing ovations in many of these same venues. I've always felt that that's one of the great things about humor, that in same way the great poet Maya Angelou said of love, "it recognizes no barriers. It jumps hurdles, leaps fences and penetrates walls." Twelve years after those incidents, I continue to do so.

It seems like over the years, anyone in comedy who happens to be anything other than a heterosexual white male has had to take this road. I think of pioneering black comics like "Moms" Mabley, Dick Gregory and Redd Foxx, all who played the chitin' circuit and often passed through and performed in places that were not so welcoming to people of color, and even risked their lives to stand up and perform, simply as they were. Trailblazing women comics like Joan Rivers, Whoopi Goldberg and Phyllis Diller also come to mind when I think of conquering the challenge of creating space for people who are rendered invisible in society—let alone comedy.

Yet, surviving and being afforded opportunities in this business continues to prove beyond challenging for most minority comics, an issue that I largely overlooked until I gained the credentials to start working weekends at comedy clubs and appearing on shows that often lead to more mainstream exposure and other things necessary to make a living as a comic, which is where I've often met resistance. For a while, seeking to work more mainstream venues, etc. the rejection was subtle "Oh, we looked at your stuff, it's good, but we don't know where to put you...wanna wait til' next June when we do our Rainbow Sherbet show?" I'd politely decline and scoff to myself, "Bitch, it's December, I have bills to pay, and I'm funny 365 days of the year, not just gay pride month."

As I continued my searches for work, the rejections became more blatant, "No, we don't bring in queer comics, and not too crazy about women comics either, sorry. I know it sounds harsh, but that's just the way it is.", "You're funny, we just don't want to risk alienating the audience.", and a more recent email, which read, "We'd rather not have comics who explore homosexual subject matter on our stage.", not to mention a late night show which told me "You're definitely funny, but we just don't think our viewers are ready for that. Good Luck." Of all the late night shows, the only one willing to give me a shot was Arsenio Hall, whose show I was in the process of getting a date on, right when he was abruptly cancelled after being renewed for a second season. You want my opinion? For one, he was the only brother in late night, and was giving opportunities to many minority artists who generally wouldn't be afforded that type of exposure anywhere else. I feel like Arsenio had a great show, during both runs, and to me, and most black folks, he's like our Johnny Carson.

Getting back to those calls and emails, I find it quite ridiculous that in some cases, LGBT subject matter and women's point of view on stage isn't afforded as many opportunities, all while some other comics (who get the opportunities and exposure, not to mention are working clubs every weekend) can stand up on stage, tell rape jokes, make fun out of abortion and traumatic events, degrade women, gay, transgender and disabled people, in some cases do racist humor, and be looked at not only as funny (as mediocre as some of them are) but never be considered "risks for alienating an audience". I don't consider myself politically correct, I feel like if that's the caliber of their humor and they're able to draw an audience to come listen, then more power to them, but the opportunity should be made to hear the other sides, no matter who we are, after all, funny is funny, and for a long time, funny has existed in the gay, women, disabled and other minority stand-up that's often overlooked, simply because we're seen as either niche or unmarketable.

The issue of diversity in comedy is beyond apparent, from the up until a while ago criticism of Saturday Night Live, which finally added a black woman to the cast after about 7 years. Then, there was Jerry Seinfeld's "Who cares about diversity in comedy? It's not the census. I have no interest in gender, race or anything like that." Comment, which to me translated into: I don't have to make an effort to see everybody." This is understandable coming from someone like him. While I respect Mr. Seinfeld and his accomplishments and contributions, he's a white man, and has never had to face the "being seen" obstacle.

This, for too long has been the general attitude directed at minorities not only in comedy, but in stage, film, television and entertainment, period, unless you're pandering to a "certain role", which I'll just call "modern day minstrelsy". I feel like in comedy, this attitude contributes to perception and this is why the lack of opportunities for minorities in this business, and statements like Mr. Seinfeld's are problematic. "Women aren't funny", so when you see one get up on stage, you get up and walk out of the room, and never get to see that she is in fact, hilarious and hear her point of view. Gay comics are usually offered "Pride Night" which most audiences don't venture out to and (although there aren't a significant number of queer comics) we get looked at like leprechauns when audiences finally see us, because some don't believe we exist (especially LGBT comics of color).

But we definitely exist, and we work hard, you have to show up and be two times funnier, and we deserve opportunities on equal platforms, as mediocre, white male comics who get free passes on rape jokes, bro references and shit humor, and enjoy mainstream exposure. After all, it shouldn't matter who you are if it's truly all about funny being funny.

Occasionally, I need inspiration, as we all sometimes do, for me, knowing that I have a connection with people, especially those who I am standing in front of onstage (and you can feel that connection in the room no matter how many people have come out to the theater), and even those who are watching that I'm not aware of, who get me, having people confide that I touch them on a deep human level, far deeper than just set up and punchline is what stirs my soul to continue creating art that nurtures. I got a letter from a teenager who came out to a family that disowned him. He told me that because of some of the things that I had joked about that were relatable, which allowed him to not only laugh, but also reflect and assured him that he wasn't the only one that had faced those horrible circumstances with his family, helped him choose not to kill himself, that made me think, hard. I've been doing this now for over a decade, people still, TODAY, even after we've had a black president, LGBT couples have been granted marriage rights by the Supreme Court, Viola Davis has made history as the first black woman to win an Emmy for Best Actress in a drama, and with more minority visibility in media and entertainment, although we could surely use more, tell me they don't want me to perform on their stages because I'm "a fag", or they're not into "that gay shit.". I get people who laugh and hang up the phone on me, and I still have to fight like a motherfucker, for a lot of the gigs that I get, and have to show up, look good, and be two or three times funnier than expected, just to make a statement. Sometimes, I ask myself "What in the hell did you get yourself into? You dumb bitch, if you were gonna come out, you should've done like everybody else, and waited until you were fully established to do that shit!"

But, things like that touch the deepest part of my heart. It lets me know that everything that I am doing is completely worth it. I'm genuinely touching people's lives, and helping to affirm people with laughter. So, if I can use my GOD given talent to not only feed myself, but nurture, and connect with people, help break down a few walls, educate, then what I am doing is not to be questioned. It's a journey. It's a journey that I'm learning from, growing from, and discovering new ways to appreciate, every single day.

9. Jackie "Moms" Mabley

I can only imagine those nights at places like the Apollo, Howard Theater and the Uptown, stages in addition to other historic venues that "Moms" Mabley ruled regularly. Almost nightly, she'd come shuffling out in a floppy hat and house coat, dragging her slippers across the stage, chewing on her gums and gazing across the audience. For minutes, she wouldn't say a word, she'd just stand there and the audience would be in hysterics, hooting, hollering and sliding out of their seats, gasping for air and wiping tears away from their eyes. Finally, at just the right moment, Moms would take the mic from the stand and open the show with one of her signature lines "You know Moms married another old man. He died, you know they say you shouldn't say nothing about the dead unless you can say something good...he's dead, good. You know children, that old man said when we buried him if I started seeing somebody else, he'd scratch his way out. So, I had him buried face down...that way, the more he scratches, the deeper he gets." The house would roar, Moms was truly a master of her craft, and in fact was once regarded as "The Funniest Woman in the World."

It bothers me that she isn't more known and that her work and history was almost lost. Thankfully, her contributions and her work ethic created the type of impact on people and influenced a new generation of black entertainers in a way that made it impossible for her legacy to die or be completely forgotten. In fact, I feel like a lot of black entertainment and stage history has been forgotten and a lot of it, simply never got the type of exposure required for enough people to recognize their artistic genius, although mainstream icons and pop culture borrowed, even stole quite a bit from those true pioneers who never got their due and suffered the harsh conditions that came along with being a performer working on the chitlin' circuit, or TOBA's black vaudeville houses. TOBA stood for 'Theater Owner's Booking Association', owned mostly by white folks providing spaces for the black community to entertain and be entertained. Many of these places were scattered throughout the Jim Crow south, where the entertainers were not allowed to stay in hotels or use dressing rooms. I've read the accounts of many performers from that era who had to change clothes in the alleyways or stairwells in between shows. As if that wasn't difficult enough, they received horrible wages and were sometimes even sexually and physically assaulted by the owners of the venues, especially if they gathered up the nerve to be vocal in their contentions with the horrors that they faced working in those venues.

One of the most inspiring things about all of this, is that even still, each and every one of those performers showed up and would give the performance of a lifetime, many, that if we were to still go back and view today, which I have on YouTube, still stand the test of time, and leaves the viewer in awe of the passion and pure skill that many of them had to dance, sing and tell jokes. While watching Whoopi Goldberg's stellar documentary on Moms Mabley, "I Got Something to Tell Ya", I heard music legend Quincey Jones summarize it all perfectly. "People would sit in the audience and go, "Damn that comedian can really dance...No you mean that dancer can tell really good jokes." They did it all, rose above their circumstances and used the stage as a platform to demonstrate the possibilities of greatness. To me, it's really sad that they rose above poverty, lack of resources, abuse, racism, lynching, dilapidated living environments and conditions and so much more, set a standard for excellence and demonstrated that night after night despite the adversity and aren't remembered for their perseverance or contributions to our culture, or that even today, so much of their work, jokes, songs, are being used and borrowed from, and despite the hell that theater and life in general was for them, that they are still robbed of their credit.

I've always felt like if Bob Hope, Milton Berle, Red Skelton and Bing Crosby can be immortalized as old Hollywood royalty, then so should Pigmeat Markham, Bert Williams and Moms Mabley because they are who they borrowed from. It's well known that many of the already successful mainstream entertainers listed above would sneak into the Apollo Theater with a pen and pad, jotting down lines and routines created by these black vaudeville stars who any especially black, or culturally educated theater lover or performer consider Apollo and black Hollywood royalty. There were other noted incidents similar to this including Pat Boone stealing songs from Little Richard, up until today with soul singing, du rags and other cultural appropriation that black and gay communities don't benefit from once our dances, slang and styles are made mainstream without us receiving any of the credit.

It really should come as no surprise that although many of us familiar with black history and the fore bearers of the black stage, that these icons have never received their due as if evidenced by the recent outcry at the lack of acknowledgement by Hollywood of stories and contributions that highlight the experiences and lives of people of color. Of course, that's nothing new, but I feel like because there are a few more black writers and directors on television like Lee Daniels, Shonda Rhimes, Tyler Perry and Ava DuVernay, pulling in major viewership in primetime and black actresses like Taraji P. Henson, Kerry Washington, Viola Davis and Angela Bassett are leading ladies in weekly television series that are outstanding and set social media abuzz with each episode, that many injustices in show business continue to fly under the radar. I feel like to a degree, many of us have become so complacent with what we feel is visibility, that we simply don't care, and fail to recognize how this is a modern version of that same history repeating itself.

While thankfully, we do have ceremonies such as the BET and NAACP awards which recognize our own, it would be nice to see some of these kinds of awards shows that do have somewhat of a voice to do so, at least in our communities, go back and make an effort to recognize a lot of these pioneers who go unacknowledged and largely unrecognized for opening doors for our current artists to be able to express themselves as they do now, although I'm sure some of our legends would cringe at what's considered honorable and talented in today's pop and entertainment culture. As a comic myself, I've studied my history and continue to do so. The history of the stage, especially for black entertainers is so rich and inspiring. Whenever I feel like I'm at a dead end or don't have any energy, or doubt myself facing the adversity that I do as a comic who happens to be black and gay, I think about these entertainers who traveled through a very segregated and terrifying Jim Crow south facing so many obstacles, see the depth and the passion and timeless quality of what they created no matter what they had to endure, and realize I have no excuses.

When I'm speaking to someone who's interested in comedy in some capacity, or even some young comics, I'm often appalled when I hear then say "Kevin Hart is the history of comedy." While I think we can all agree that as a black man in Hollywood first, then a comic, he's accomplished a level of success and opportunity that I'm sure and have witnessed listening to some backstage conversations, the cause of envy for many in the business who've worked just as hard and perhaps are even funnier, but have been overlooked. Infact, I'm sure that he's even inspired a new generation of aspiring comics, because since his success, and going to movie theaters seeing trailers for every upcoming comedy or action film starring or co-starring Kevin Hart, I've seen more and more young people aspire to be comedians, when, years ago when I started, no one really cared much about being a comic. At some showcase and open mic nights, the host would have the three or four of us who were on the show, to come back for encore sets because not enough people had signed up, or cared to get onstage, and honestly, back then if you weren't funny they'd boo you off the stage, or on a night where the crowd was more hostile, would throw chicken bones and beer cans at you. I think every nightclub venue, especially black ones was reminiscent of The Apollo. To be honest, I really miss those days. It kept those of us who were there, passionate and dedicated and the people who shouldn't be up there off. There are some brilliant comics coming up and who've been around for a while, but on the other hand, with social media apps like Instagram and Vine, there is a lot of crap getting through just because they can get followers and all the clubs think about is money, and not talent. However, I'll digress.

I guess the biggest concern about the issue of our history and where we are now is that so much of it is disrespected and overlooked. I've never understood why it seems like the careers of many of our legends pass when they do, unless an artist that they've inspired or mentored in some capacity take us back to remind their audiences of where something has come from, or where or how art has been inspired by a pioneer or event that occurred before. This is one reason why I'm so respectful of and adamant about constantly making sure we remember people like Moms. I still remember learning about her when I was a young, gay adolescent, making my way through puberty and figuring out who I was growing into as a person of both of those identities and sneaking into gay clubs or visiting gay friends, queens in their late 30's, 40's and a couple of them in their early to mid-50's, chain smoking cigarettes and playing spades, sitting at a dinette table and reading each other to filth. "Girl, don't come in here throwing me shade. You weren't throwing shade last week when that piece of trade kicked your dry ass to the curb and you drove over here crying and sniffling, looking like Moms Mabley." The room would explode with laughter as the person who'd just been read, would throw down their card and roll their eyes. It was funny to hear because of how quick they were, and the wit and put downs. I'd hear her name quite a bit, but I had no idea that she was a real person.

You see, I'd grown up being reared by southern folks and there had been quite a few expressions that I'd heard that sounded catchy, but were also too ridiculous to actually mean anything, like "the man in the moon", "drunk as a skunk", "high as Kudi Brown" and "stinking to beat the band." They made me laugh too, but I knew they didn't mean anything and when I heard folks referring to "Moms Mabley", I thought she was just another expression in the category of sayings. I'd hear it constantly, when a homeless woman with a floppy hat on, toothless, shaking a cup outside of 7-11 would be begging for spare change, someone would go "Look at her, sitting out here, looking like Moms Mabley." It wasn't until I started venturing down to DuPont Circle in DC exploring the gay book and record stores, namely a now defunct shop "Melody Records", browsing for albums by some of my favorite divas, Patti LaBelle, Chaka Khan, Tina Turner, then over to Mahalia Jackson and right near there, I saw it "Moms Mabley".

I couldn't believe it. I jumped and flipped to see the selections they offered behind that tab with her name on it. There were two CD's, one of an old lady in a floppy hat, sitting on a chair, holding a microphone on stage at the Apollo, called "I Got Something to Tell Ya!" and another with a sketch of maybe what was a headshot of the same woman and the title "Comedy Ain't Pretty". I had a moment, looking at her pictures, somewhat in a state of awe, because I didn't realize she was a real person. This was before Google, Wikipedia and all of those different search engines that became available to provide rich sources of information on people and things. As I write about this, I'm thinking that's another reason why it caught me so off guard. I do remember thinking, "Damn! Well, the man in the moon must be real too, and maybe I should look around to see if I can find a Kudi Brown album?"

I snagged one of the albums, and carried it up to the cash register, paid the $7 for it, broke the wrapper off and popped the disc into my CD player. I rode the Metro home that night, listening to the content, enamored by her gravelly voice, raunchiness and every double entendre. It was cool to hear a woman who you'd think of as somebody's great, great grandmother express her interest in young men who were three times younger than her, and loving a man who "knows what he wants", and how she'd be "happy to give it to him." I also listened as she used that same wit and passion to lecture those audiences on things like racism, sexism and ageism. Hearing things like that made me realize how long black women have been vocal about being proud to be women, regardless of how black, poor, ugly, nappy headed or whatever it was that society tried to use as a paintbrush and make stigmatize them as or with, take that paintbrush and use it to tell that same society to kiss their asses and have society love them for it.

It's funny because for so long, these have been the ultimate expressions of women's liberation and feminism, but none of them got the credit or respect for those things. Although I'm a man, one of my favorite speeches is Sojourner Truth's "Aint I a Woman?" a speech about a woman's strength and even the challenges that one faced being a woman of color. I listen to old routines by other lady comics like LaWanda Page, on a microphone, in front of an audience, using language that would make a sailor blush, talking freely of her love for sex, dick, drinking liquor and smoking weed, or reading the biography of women like Harriet Tubman, carrying a rifle and leading over a thousand slaves to freedom on the Underground Railroad—it makes you realize that in many ways black women are the true pioneers of women's lib and definition of feminism, which is ultimately about honoring women's strength and resilience in a world that has looked down on them because of their gender and in the cases of the queens listed above, also because of their color.

This is one reason why I've always looked at black women especially, as superheroes. I think they possess a certain magic, power and grace, wit, resilience and love, all wrapped up in them that you can't find anywhere else in the world. Among the many things that made "Moms" so special, is looking at her career as the only black woman of note being in the business of comedy, on vaudeville stages in the 1920's, on through the 50's becoming one of the highest paid headliners at the Apollo Theater, making $10,000 a week, and in the late 60's, up until her passing in the mid 70's, mainstream stages including Carnegie Hall. She matched and surpassed the wits of her beloved male counterparts and did it in a floppy hat, in a housedress and slippers, smiling a toothless grin. She was one of the first to stand in front of white audiences and talk about racism and segregation, challenging the discrimination that existed so blatantly and with humor and I'm sure disarming those audiences not just with how funny she was, but also the image of a homeless, old woman. The fact that in real life, she was a butch lesbian who dressed super dapper, and would dress up in the costume to do the act, and growing into the character as she actually got older, speaks to the kind of comic genius she was.

Maybe "Moms" never realized it, but by doing that, she challenged respectability politics, showing up in a way that we knew our grandmothers from around the way to do. She never tried to change her speech or appearance to make anyone comfortable, or to fit in herself. In that floppy hat, sitting in that chair, chewing on her gums, she challenged the ideas of what glamourous is, every time she surveyed her audience lecherously accusing young men in the audience of lusting after her. "Moms" was sex positive when she expressed her disinterest in older men because she was busy showing you "a young man who could, for every old man who couldn't", and she showed us what it looked like to show up, be yourself, say what you have to say, and have a right to be loved. She obviously was loved because she was a star of the Apollo and stayed on the lips of people who absolutely adored her. Of course, some of those would be gay men, who I'm sure have drawn strength watching someone like "Moms" persevere in spite of racism, appearance, where she came from or her gender, in an age and business, dominated by all men. Being LGBT, and more specifically an LGBT person of color and facing the issues that we do, being both gay and of color, you know first-hand what persevering in spite of, looks like. Moms Mabley is a great example of all of that, as are many gay icons.

I got booked to perform at a college in Bronxville, NY. It wasn't quite upstate New York, but it was close enough to White Plains, NY where she lived and is buried, to be determined to make an extra trip out of it since I was so close, and go visit her. After about 45 minutes of searching, I found her headstone in one of the plots at Ferncliff Cemetery. It was a sunny, but freezing cold December afternoon, I could barely move my fingers and the chill in the air was starting to get the best of me, and I was already kind of annoyed, because the girl on the bus ride there, sitting behind me popped gum for the entire half hour I was on there, anyone who knows me, knows, that sound drives me crazy! Once I saw the name Jackie "Moms" Mabley, it instantly warmed me up and boosted my spirits. I felt as though I'd been hugged by an elder relative that I hadn't seen in person, but had heard so much about. I knelt down, running my fingers across her name on the headstone, a smile grew across my face. I teased her for not even being buried next to any old men, then thanked her for everything and had a personal conversation with her. Physically, of course she wasn't there, but I could feel her warmth, her love and thoughts of what meeting her in the flesh would've been like flickered through my mind. It was almost as if I could feel her being proud of and encouraging me, jokingly smiling that wide, toothless grin, looking me over, half lecherously and saying "Baby, you know I like young men."

10. Mister

I've always wondered what it would've been like to have a conversation with my father. What would he think of me? What would his stories be? I sometimes wonder how much I look, or act like him. Growing up, I would get very angry at my mother whenever she said things to me like "I swear, sometimes you act just like your father." In fact, whenever she said that, I'd get offended because although my mother, or people who knew and shared their stories about him with me, never straight up trashed him, the stigma surrounding black men who leave women with children stung growing up. Today, with reality television, and the fact that so many in my generation grew up without their dads, having both parents in the house isn't such a big deal now. When I was growing up, if you didn't have a father around, it seemed like people expected the worse for you. From your sexuality to career and life choices, I think any of us who grew up knowing that we had a father perfectly capable of being in our lives, but opting not to were pushed hard by our mothers, aunt, grandmothers, older siblings or whoever raised us, to be strong and prove everybody wrong. In many cases, depending on who else was there, we became the men of the house, even at very young and impressionable ages.

Growing up, I saw my mother only seriously date two men. One of those men was a deacon in the church, and then a couple years later when we moved to Maryland, she met a security guard who liked to drink and use my body as punching bag practice. If I remember correctly, before he started to show his true colors, they hit it off immediately and quite well. I remembered the first guy because he came to visit, they'd hang out after church, but I don't remember him talking to or paying much attention to me. I do remember a restaurant on Benning Road in DC that we'd frequent often called "The Chef's Table". It was the place to go, and the folks would be in there dressed to the nines every Sunday. I was about four, and remember a couple of times when he'd help prop me up in a booster seat so that I could eat with them, and he may have given me a baseball or toy truck, but he never made it a point to have much of a relationship with me. He clearly was in that relationship to be with my mother only, I was just an accessory to the scenario. I still never thought much of it, although I do remember cutting up in class a couple times, or breaking something in the house and my mom would ask him to talk to me. He'd simply say "Stop giving your mom a hard time, because then you make it harder for me." I had no idea what that meant, and never paid it much attention. I'd just walk away, lost in my own little world and start breaking things or fall into some kind of other mischief again.

A couple years later, my mother started seeing the other guy, who seemed to begrudge the fact that I was around and that he had to split her attention with me. From the start, he was an asshole, stepping in to fill a father role, albeit a very poor one and doing so with an iron fist. We all went to church together every Sunday, and afterwards, we'd go out to have dinner, usually at

Red Lobster, because that's where all the bourgeoisie black folks went back in the day. One Sunday afternoon, we'd gotten out of church and stopped past a Post Office. My mom got out to buy a stamp from the lobby machine and use the payphone, and left us in the car alone together—so obviously, she trusted him. Usually, she'd leave me in there alone and warn me not to open the door for anybody. The funny thing is that back then, kids got left in cars all the time, but you rarely heard of any dying because it got too hot in the car, or there was some other emergency, we were smart enough to open the door, and get out. We'd just have to take the ass whooping for getting out, but we didn't die in cars. I'd sit in there, left to my own devices and imagination, usually playing around in the cigarette tray, which for many black folks who didn't smoke, doubled as a coin box. I'd open it and run my fingers through the loose change, occasionally pulling out a nickel or dime, and keeping it. I'd done that for years and it had never been a problem. So, when I reached across from the backseat and opened it up, and he pushed my hand out of it and slammed the box close, you can probably imagine how much that hurt my feelings—and yes, made me mad even. What had I done? And why was this man putting his hands on me?

I paused for a second and looked at him, then opened up the change box and started playing in it again, which is when he popped my hand, firmly slammed the box shut again and covered it with his closed fist. When I tried to open it again, he took that same fist and punched me in the chest. The air left my body and I went flying into the backseat, I'd never had a grown man hit me before and I knew I hadn't done anything wrong. I'm not sure if it was because

I'd learned early that if someone ever hit you, you hit them back, or if it was to fight in honor of my beloved loose change, but all I know is with all the rage a 6-year-old boy could have, I launched myself at the back of his head. Once I latched hold to it, I wailed, screamed, punched and scratched as if my life depended on it. Yet, to no avail, I was a mere baby, up against a 32-year-old man who did security for a living. He handled me quite quickly, and as he was holding me down by my head in the backseat, my mom returned to the car. She was dumbfounded. She'd left us in the car for five minutes, and came back to World War III. I don't remember the conversation completely, but I do remember her trying to drive and listen to what happened, while he and I screamed at each other and nearly came to blows again. Finally, at a stoplight, she ordered me back into my seat belt and demanded that we stop fighting. He was with us until I was 11 and that was our relationship the entire time, somehow, I still managed to get used to it and even learned to respect him and his authority in the house, at one time, I think I was flat out scared of him.

I never called him "Dad", or step dad, I called him by his name, Brian. One day, I guess I was in the third grade and remember walking into the doors of my school, the aroma of fresh pancakes, sausage and French toast greeting me upon my arrival. I wondered what was so special about the morning as I walked into the cafeteria for breakfast. This wasn't the typical morning where the students came in grabbing boxes of cereal and cartons of milk, hollering and signifying, playing the dozens from across cafeteria tables, while two or three administrators scrambled to keep order. This morning was calm, and slightly formal. I looked around and the cafeteria was filled with many of the boys from our school, some I was friends with, who of course I looked around to see if I could locate, and as I surveyed the tables, noticed that they all seemed to be sitting next to boys with hairy faces, who looked like big versions of them. I had no idea why it was so different, or what was happening, until one of the administrators came up, placing a gentle hand on my shoulders, leaned into my ear and asking "Sampson, you look lost this morning. Did you bring your father? You guys want some sausage and pancakes?" I looked around the room a bit more then replied "No, I just want some breakfast." He smiled, "Well, this morning if you didn't bring your dad, you have to eat at one of these tables in the corner." He handed me a blue flier with the words "Bring your father to school day." That listed monthly dates that you could bring your dad with you to eat breakfast.

I wandered over to where the breakfast was being served and got my Frosted Flakes and milk, then over to the two designated tables for those of us without our fathers present sat. There weren't many of us, but those of us who sat there seemed to stare at what was going on, full of curiosity about what we were seeing. That was my first time seeing that, but I remember once a month, sitting there watching. I remember a couple of the students bringing in a different daddy each breakfast, and later during the day, overhearing nosey teachers and the two shady lunch ladies in the hallway call out "Your daddy looked different today!" I never had any idea what was going on, until after the first day I carried the flier home, and asked Brian if he'd go with me to the next one, which is when he took the blue flier, looking it over while rubbing his belly (which I hated watching him do it always made me wonder if he was pregnant), and handed me the paper back saying "I'm not going to that. I'm not your father."

That didn't hurt my feelings or upset me any, in fact, I still had no idea what the hell was going on. I thought my life was perfectly okay until that night, I asked my mom why I didn't have a dad to take to the breakfast. That's when I found out that he wasn't around. Full of curiosity, I had other questions like "Where is he?!" I'm not sure if my mom was ready to have that conversation, but she summoned the courage that I'm sure she needed to pull from a very deep and emotional place to tell me that he'd left us and stopped speaking to her, shortly after I was born. "Why?" I questioned. "That's just what he did. He had another family, and when I found out, he didn't want you to be a part of it." She still didn't go too far into details, either because she was still dealing with her own emotions about it, or maybe because she didn't think I'd totally understand her explanation, possibly both reasons, but considering the circumstances, she did the very best that she could. I remember sitting on the floor in front of her in the living room, which is where she always laid the deep shit on me and watched as she pulled out a photo album. After a few seconds, she pulled out a polaroid picture and handed it to me, and told me who the man staring back was, "That's your father."

I'll never forget pulling that picture up to eye level, looking at every detail, as he seemed to look at me the same way, as if he was getting his first good look at his son, too. He was dark brown, with a Jheri curl tucked neatly under a straw hat as he peered over the rim of his square framed glasses, smiling in a vintage denim jacket. "That's my daddy?" My mother nodded, and I can still remember the image as clear as that day, and that was years ago. I sat the picture down on the floor in front of me as I listened to her carefully offer an explanation of some of the events that had occurred, from him leaving her right after she gave birth to me, because he had another family and he didn't want to deal with the additional responsibility. She told me about how he drove her home after the hospital cleared me to come home, and how after that, he'd disappeared into the night and stopped coming around. Although, every now and again, he'd drop a pack of diapers or leave some baby formula at the back door, but he never came back around to see us, or try to get to know his new kid. I took another look at that picture, then handed it back. I really didn't know what to think, but I was definitely intelligent enough to understand what had happened and even though I was so young, rationalize why he'd left. Perhaps the fact that he'd also gone to jail allowed me to come to a place where I was able to accept the fact that there was nothing I could do about him being gone, and for damn sure, neither could he. He was pressing license plates somewhere in Virginia.

My mom pulled out a full page news article about a crime that he'd attempted to commit and how when he, a real estate mogul in the DC-Maryland area was busted by an undercover officer, "took off running like a scolded dog." That had to be some serious running. The article elaborated on the other details of the scenario including how he was apprehended and put in jail for close to twenty years. Although I understood the details, at that age, I think I was so preoccupied with my own interests that none of it ever affected me emotionally right away. As far as my "step dad", Brian, was concerned, I knew he had to have quite a bit of contempt for me, to constantly remind me that he wasn't my dad the way that he did. Not to mention, never made any effort to develop any kind of relationship with me, I remember, we'd be right in the kitchen standing next to each other, and we wouldn't part lips as to even breathe in the direction of each other. I do know that perhaps if he'd spent as much time working to make a connection with me as he did wailing on me, punching me in the chest, kicking me in the privates and keeping me on strict punishments, that we could have gotten along well, maybe still have a close bond, even though he and my mother have been long broken up.

Til this day, I wouldn't care to see him again. I've emotionally forgiven him for terrorizing me at such a young age, but I'll never forget any of the cruel things that he did or how badly he used to treat me. As I got a little older, a part of me resented my father, and looked forward to him dying. I planned to celebrate by having a cocktail party over wherever he was buried. I couldn't help but wonder that maybe, if he was around, I wouldn't have had a guy who hated my guts, even though he was with my mother, treating me like trash and maybe someone would've been able to take me out to play football or basketball, and just be cool, riding around town.

I wasn't the most masculine little boy, and was often accused of being "a little soft in the toes." I did play with dolls and EZ bake ovens, when my mom wasn't taking them from me and tossing them in the trash or breaking them up with hammers, but I still liked to do things that other boys my age did, I loved riding dirt bikes, playing in the mud, even learned how to play basketball and football and got more than my share of scraped up and skinned knees and elbows. I loved wrestling, because if anything, it gave me an excuse to put my body on another boy's. I'd known that I was attracted to men, way before this point, or that I'd known anything about my dad bailing and then being sent to jail. Of course, there was my mom, other women in the community, including the teachers and babysitters, my peers and a few men from the church and barbershop who felt that young boys not having their father, or a strong male figure in their life made them gay, punks or weak, but even before I was able to define sexuality, I knew that something was "different" about me, even though I didn't know what that "different" thing was. I also noticed a couple of other boys at school and church who also were "different" although they had both of their parents and great relationships, quite a few that I envied even, with their dads.

When I wasn't being called "sweet", or "punks", I dealt with those people, and not to mention news statistics and reports that young, black men who grew up without dads, usually ended up on the streets selling dope, dead or in jail. I do think my mom tried to be hard on me because of that, but I never had any interest in being a hoodlum, didn't get into many fights, and excelled in most of my classes when I wasn't cutting up, being a clown and actually paid attention long enough to do my work and not get put out of class. By the time I was around 11, my mom and I had become homeless, sleeping in our 90' Geo

Storm, Greyhound stations, bus stops and when we could scrape the money up for it, a hotel. Some of those late nights, crammed up in that stuffy car, fidgeting uncomfortably, I'd occasionally think of my dad and what life would be like if he were around or even sending money. Hell, he owned property, he could've put us up somewhere, but those weren't the cards that we were dealt.

I finally saw my father in person, twice when I was 15. Once, my mom and I were on a crowded Metro train and stood a few feet away from him, when she noticed him and tried to move us through the car to get to him. The train was definitely at capacity, and it just wasn't meant to be, by the time we got to the spot where he was, he'd gotten off the train, and seemed to had disappeared again into thin air, a skill that he'd seemed to had mastered quite well just 15 years before. I didn't see him again until a few months later, my mom had taken him to court to try and fight for child support, yet to no avail. She'd gone to about three different hearings and the judge refused to rule because he said something about my dad not being mentally competent, which I don't know how true it was. I do know that he was a very shrewd man who did what he had to do in order to hold on to what he had. If that meant showing up with a bottle of meds, mumbling incoherently when he was asked questions, then that's what he did.

My mother didn't play about me missing days from school, so I only went to one of the dates, which is the first and only time that I ever got a good look at or completely looked my father over. I don't remember his face very well, but I do remember his frame, tall and slender, head hung low under a tan fedora. We never made eye contact, and he never said a word to me, even as I sat a few feet away from him. I even remember my mom having me write our names on the court petition for her, and me standing next to where he was sitting. He sat there, with his head still hung, peering at me briefly from under the brim of his hat, then turning and looking at the wall in front of him. I didn't even get to see his face in the court room, as hard as I tried. As quickly as he slid in at the beginning of the hearing, he slipped back out at the end, again, quickly and vanishing without a trace, the way that I always knew him to do and one of the only things that I know about him. My mother used to come home and tell me these stories about them arguing outside of the courtroom after hearings, and I wondered why I couldn't be so lucky the day that I was there, to see him up close, hear his voice, hear him cuss, hear his wit, even if it did come in the form of an excuse as to why he was absent from my life, but, I got nothing.

There was one more hearing that my mom went to, before finally, a few weeks after that, she called me at school to tell me that he had died. I remember when everybody would buy the newspapers and look through the obituaries, I can only imagine the response my mother had when she opened the paper and saw his name and picture listed. I do know, when I went to the school office and picked up the receiver, she simply told me that he'd died and not to tell anybody. I went back to class, not knowing what to think about the news I'd just gotten. In the back of my head, I did start making plans to find out where he was buried so I could go and pop bottles and celebrate, but when what happened started to sink in, I started to feel differently. I mostly felt empty, and spent a while spaced out. My mind wandered all over the place, and things really set in when we went to his wake in Maryland. I'll never forget walking into the church and the "hush falling over Jerusalem", as we walked down the aisle to view his body. I saw a few folks whispering and nudging each other, and it's funny how even then, in 2003, the church and country folk still found it taboo to accept, or openly acknowledge children that a man had outside of his marriage, or how badly the woman was looked at if she had the child out of wedlock. Thankfully, I'd had enough experience with church shade, so I was well prepared in what to expect.

I just sat there in a pew in the middle of the church, watching his casket and the service, all while some of the people in the church seemed to look at me like I was the plague. It's funny how much a little time can change folks, because sometimes I think, yeah, I sat there feeling cold and a little awkward, but if it were me now, I would've gone up there and gotten on that microphone during the reflections portion of the service and said something. Perhaps that would've made me feel a little different some weeks later, maybe better, maybe worse, but all I know is that the anger and disappointment of never having the chance to have a conversation with him set in and started to haunt me, day and night. Even if my words and face, the fact that I was a part of his fabric weren't enough to bind him, then simply growing up and making a success out of myself would've been enough, just to let him know that I was still okay. The reality of all of it set in, and that's when feelings of rejection, even some hatred started to seep into those feelings that I had and found me having crying fits daily. He was never mine, but losing him hurt, and although I moved on, I'm still not sure if I ever got over him never wanting me, and no matter how close I ever got, always vanishing and finally disappearing forever.

I sometimes think, maybe as tough as having to adjust to life despite the rejection was, it could've made me just as vulnerable. One of my biggest fears has always been abandonment, and I've found myself in a few situations that I shouldn't have been in, all because I wanted to make somebody happy enough to stay around, even when I knew they really didn't want to, or blaming myself for having to let someone go. Those have left some of the deepest scars that you could imagine, while at the same time the tough skin of growing up feeling and learning that, made it easy for me to absorb those kinds of emotional blows but never get hurt too badly. It's really sad to see people who experience those kinds of emotional traumas, but never get to heal enough to function quite properly.

I never got a chance to feel sorry for myself, and always placed in situations where if I didn't keep a level of emotional stability, then everything would fall apart which isn't something that I, or my mother (especially when we were living on the street) could afford. I'm not sure if I ever quite want to know exactly how I feel about that scenario, the rejection, or the fact that my old man kicked the bucket without me ever getting to talk to him one on one. I'm not sure if he even would have, or how I'd feel now, walking around, going about my life knowing he was walking around too, and that we weren't talking.

Now that he's gone, all I can do is imagine, which I sometimes find myself doing. What would a conversation between us be like? Would I listen to him? How we he feel about me being gay? Would I notice any traits that we share? For me, the hard part sometimes is when every now and then, depending on the day, or a certain way that I wear my hat, I catch a glimpse of him in the mirror, and I'll stop and stare at him, a few questions will pop into my head, sometimes, I'll just stand there, surprised at who I see, until I move my head or readjust my face, and watch him disappear just as quickly as I've always known him to. As you move through life, you learn how to understand and accept things and move on, which is what I've done, but of course, from time to time, his name floats into my head, or I'll see a man playing with young son in a park or at a basketball court and I'll ask myself what that would've been like. Eventually, I just keep on with my life, no longer feeling the resentment, rejection or anger, but wondering if he knows, wherever he is, what I strive to be in life, who I am and how proud I try to make him every day, even though he was never around.

About the Author

Sampson McCormick is an experience, a down to earth comedic force of nature, and for well over a decade has been one of the most celebrated LGBT comics working. He's been named "One of the Funniest Comics" by Huffington Post, BuzzFeed and The Advocate.

In addition to lending his voice to causes including conversations on race and sexuality in America, eradicating homophobia and youth homelessness, he is a highly sought after entertainer who has headlined venues including The historic Howard Theater in DC, where he made history as the first black, gay entertainer to headline the venue, The San Francisco Punch Line, The Comedy Factory in Hollywood and the Kennedy Center for the Performing Arts.

His comedy offers riveting and fresh takes on race, sexuality, politics and religion—you know, all those things you aren't supposed to talk about in polite company.